Mary Magd
Lost Goddess, Lost
Gospel

Jan McDonald

www.capallbann.co.uk

Mary Magdalene Lost Goddess, Lost Gospel

ISBN 186163 252 5

Cover design by Paul Mason
Cover photograph by Jan McDonald of a stained glass window in Kilmore Church on the Isle of Mull

Published by:

Capall Bann Publishing
Auton Farm
Milverton
Somerset
TA4 1NE

Contents

Rev. Jan McDonald

Introduction

The Mary Magdalene story has all the ingredients of a blockbusting detective novel; fallen hero, exiled heroine, conspiracy theories and ecclesiastical cover ups, as we can see in the inspired and stunningly brilliant *Da Vinci Code* by Dan Brown, whilst being a work of fiction some of his references are founded in what we know as Gnostic truths. The heroine is denied, downgraded and her true status hidden from Christians and non-Christians alike for twenty centuries, but like all good detective stories, 'the truth will out' by way of carefully hidden clues if we look in the right places.

Our exiled heroine has been silenced by mainstream Christianity for too long, she has been painted as a prostitute by the Roman Catholic Church for centuries without justification or foundation which it has now seen fit to acknowledge and we can follow those hidden clues in the cold light of reality.

My early years found me attending church regularly but without too much enthusiasm for the dry and somewhat frightening portrayal of a scary God and his redeeming Son. Even back then there was a feeling of 'something missing', which evolved into a search for a spirituality that had a greater meaning for me personally and this led my footsteps to the path of the Goddess in paganism. There I found the duality and sacred union that I had searched for and for many years that is where I called my spiritual home. Yet there was still that certain 'something' that was missing.

Many times on my pagan journey I found myself thinking of Christ and what he had meant to me. I thought back to the days of reciting endless liturgies in a cold church, words that had meant nothing to me and left me empty; but I had retained a quiet heartache for the man so vilely treated, who had died such a terrible death for, if what I was told was true, me and my soul and every other soul on this earth.

And there it was; the proverbial head of the nail. Jesus Christ had been a living man, acting as a physical vehicle for the Divine, who interacted with people who had existed, had eaten and drunk and lived with people who bore witness to it, and there was documentary and archaeological evidence to support it.

This was something that was different from the pagan Gods and Goddesses which were archetypes, for the most part born of the human psyche to explain natural phenomena, to live in mythology. They simply had not been flesh and blood. Christ had lived, died, and more importantly, risen. His victory over death was special because unlike the archetypes of mythology, he actually did rise from the dead and ascend.

Ascension is the name of the game now, as this world is challenged to its foundations. Christ taught the blueprint for ascension and hidden within the clues in the gospels and other writings contemporary with His days we find, time and time again, the reference to sacred union as part of the plan. So I had gone full circle but still with a yearning for the Goddess figure in Christianity. The Roman Catholic Church paid lip service to the Goddess in the form of the Virgin Mary, but she was not in place as the partner to God. I had quickly learned during my sojourn with paganism that a God had a Goddess, there was always a Yin to the Yang and vice versa. In creation, there had to be a male and a female element. Even in hermaphrodites there was a male and female combined in one entity. So where was the Christian Goddess figure hiding?

Then, two things happened simultaneously. Firstly, I read an article that denounced the Roman Catholic teaching that Mary, the mother of Christ had been forever virgin. Even in the Bible there were several references to his Mother and his brothers and sisters. Throughout all denominations of Christianity the common source is the Catholic Church and its teachings, and here was the first of many mis-teachings. The evidence was concrete. Apparently there had been a mistranslation at best, a manipulation of the truth at worst. And if one fact had suffered this fate, then what of others?

The same article referred to the lost gospels, writings contemporary with those of the four gospels in the bible, that had been deliberately axed from the canon (the accepted gospels of Matthew, Mark, Luke and John) when Emperor Constantine had declared himself Pope and had set up the Council of Nicea to decide what was to become available information for the entire Roman Empire and what was to be hidden because of its dangerous content. Dangerous for the Roman Catholic Church and its power structures and hierarchies, that is. Now these gospels had been found and were available for all to read, one of which was the Gospel of Mary Magdalene. Apparently, Constantine's hatchet job hadn't been thorough enough. Some of his fears were about to be realised. Big time.

Here I stood on the dividing line that all at once became clear. The Bible in its original form was not the Bible that we were being handed. The victim of mistranslation and mishandling, in some instances the alteration of one single word obliterated the actual meaning of what was after all the word of God. The original gospels had been written in Aramaic, the language that Jesus spoke. Later they were translated into Hebrew, then to Greek and onwards to Latin, followed by medieval English. Chinese whispers comes to mind.

Secondly, I came across a book called *The Woman with the Alabaster Jar* by Margaret Starbird, a brilliant and heart-wrenching account of evidence that provided me with what I had searched for. A Goddess figure in Christianity. According to this author, Jesus, it seemed, had taken a wife, Mary Magdalene. She had become the Sophia to his Logos. There were tears in my eyes as I gratefully devoured every word. If this were true, how would that gentle, peace loving, peace teaching Son of God, whose main message was one of love, feel to see his bride denied? And not only that, the author aims to show that there was evidence that there was a child and that the blood line of Christ still existed. This would only have been possible with a bride who was fully human.

The Magdalene story began to unfold.

In recent years documents have been retrieved from millennia of dust to shed light on this most enigmatic of characters and elevate her to her rightful status; that of Lost Bride of Christ about to return and reclaim her throne. It had not been the intention of Jesus to create a new religion in his name, merely to bring enlightenment and truth to those that were open enough to listen to him. In fact, some of the travesties which have been committed in his name must, I fear, make him very sad.
Christianity accounts for almost two thirds of the world's religion and yet it has been delivered down the centuries as incomplete and distorted into a false patriarchal belief system

but whilst its roots were in the patriarchal line, it was radically changed by Christ himself by his new covenants, his crucifixion and subsequent resurrection and ascension. A Roman emperor and his appointed mortal men, some centuries later, decided what was to become the 'accepted' doctrine of Christianity with complete disregard for the truth, the whole truth and nothing but the truth. What we are left with is a watered down and distorted version of the amazing teachings of the Son of God. A dilution which has done no-one any favours.

Now is the time, however, that mankind is searching for the truth and thanks to many years of hard slog, soul searching, research and brave publishing, those hidden clues are coming to light to bring radiance to something wonderful. God in Man with His Bride in place. I can make no claim to that original hard slog and I am no Hercule Poirot, but I do have a burning passion for the Magdalene and I have done my best to bring her story into yet another volume, ever conscious of the gratitude that is due to those who have sacrificed much to bring light into the dark void of misunderstanding.

I have not written this text from a standpoint of undermining Christianity. I am in fact now an ordained Christian minister and it is this fact alone and my deep love for Jesus Christ that I seek to better understand His relationship with someone who was clearly a key figure in His life and ministry. If the Magdalene was, as is currently being hotly debated, his wife or consort then certainly, to deny this further is an offence to the one we seek to serve. If in fact she was more than that, the Sophia to His Logos, the embodiment of the Goddess to His Godhead then indeed we have a duty to restore the feminine divine to Her rightful place in Christianity.

I have traced the Magdalene's footsteps through Scotland and France, her hidden shrines and disguised places of worship and have tried to bring those lost gospels into today's perspective. This is the time of the Age of Aquarius when male and female will find balance in us and in the divine and true healing will be brought about at the core of our souls.

Follow me on the journey to the Goddess figure of Christianity, to The Magdalene.

Roman rule and Roman Church obliterate your name
They designate you 'sinner', lost in earthly shame
But you are the Magdal-Eder, the Watchtower of the Flock
Despite the great dismissal by the one He called the Rock.
Time now to take your rightful place at the centre of the stage
Time to shine your gentle light at the dawning of an age
We hear your voice and see your face; the veil is torn aside
Welcome home O Magdalene as Jesus Christ's lost Bride

Chapter One

The Magdalene of the Gospels

Penitent prostitute, Mary of Bethany, Wife of Christ, Apostle to the Apostles, the First Apostle; will the real Mary Magdalene please stand?

Who is Mary Magdalene and why is her true identity so important over two thousand years after her death?

If we are to believe what the Roman Catholic and other orthodox churches would have us believe, Mary Magdalene was a penitent prostitute from whom Jesus cast out seven demons, who became a subsequent follower of Christ and who anointed his feet with precious oil and was present, according to Matthew and Mark but not Luke, at the resurrection.

So let's start there. Let's examine more closely the words of the Bible as we have been permitted to receive them. We are told by The Church that the Bible is the true and inspired word of God; therefore it must be a reliable source of inform- ation. In its original form, that is. Subsequent translations are not covered by that declaration, it's the great get-out clause. If we look at all mentions of the Magdalene within the canonical writings and follow with logic the references and implications, we will come to a reasonably reliable idea of her true status which can later be fleshed out by the recent discovery of documents which were excluded from the canon by the Roman Church back at the Council of Nicea.

Firstly, and most importantly, nowhere in any of the gospels or elsewhere in the New Testament does it say that Mary Magdalene was a prostitute. She was described in the gospel as a sinner. It is the assumptions of subsequent readers that because she was designated a sinner and a woman, then it followed that the nature of her sin was one of adultery or prostitution. Given the patriarchal, masculine dominated opinions of the times, which had been adopted by the Roman Catholic and subsequently the Anglican churches, this would have been their obvious reaction, however erroneous.

Art and literature have all portrayed Mary Magdalene as carrying an alabaster jar. The first biblical reference to this is Matthew's gospel in chapter six where Jesus is anointed in Bethany. Confusion has arisen here as to whether the Mary named here was in fact Mary Magdalene, or as we will see, Mary of Bethany, one and the same 'Mary'. Jesus is so touched by this act, which has a deeper significance than is first seen, that he instructs the disciples to tell it everywhere they go in memory of her. She appears next at the crucifixion scene of Matthew, where she heads the list of women present when all of the disciples had fled in fear of their own lives. Matthew tells us towards the end of his gospel that Mary Magdalene also accompanied Joseph of Arimathea when he placed Christ's body in the tomb and of course we find her alone in the garden with Christ after his resurrection.

To understand fully the implications of what we read in the four canonical gospels we need to understand the politics and Jewish laws of the day. As far as religious practice went, women were not even allowed into the holy places in the temple. It was a man's prerogative to publicly speak about and listen to the Holy Law, so when Mary sat at Jesus' feet in awe and absorbing his every teaching, she was rebuked by her sister Martha and asked to return to the kitchen where she belonged. It was against Jewish law for a woman to touch a man in public let alone anoint his feet and wipe them with her hair. The gospels show us that the word of Mary Magdalene, when she returned to the disciples with the good news of the resurrection, was treated with scorn and disbelief. Further, in the Gospel of Mary Magdalene, we find Peter using the words, 'the ramblings of a woman', showing his true feelings for this mere woman who Jesus had chosen to be the first witness of the resurrection. Repeatedly we hear Peter ask, 'Why did He love this woman more than us?'

Plainly, even in the canonical gospels this is a very special woman to Jesus and the relationship, although not disclosed, is so obviously an intimate one.

We see Peter's hand so clearly in the Roman Catholic Church which he founded, in its structure and doctrine, so it is little wonder then that the true relationship of the Magdalene to Christ has been denied for so many centuries given the tensions between the two. But that is only the superficial view. The entire principle of Apostolic succession on which the authority of the Roman Church rests in coming from Peter as the First Apostle, the one to whom Christ appeared first after the resurrection is completely and utterly flawed. We are told quite categorically in Mark 16:9 (NIV) *'When Jesus rose early on the first day of the week, he appeared first to Mary Magdalene, out of whom he had driven seven demons. She went and told those that had been with Him and were mourning and weeping. When they heard that Jesus was alive and that she had seen Him, they didn't believe it.'* We can almost see Peter's scorn as he cannot believe that Jesus would appear first to a woman and thereby bestow upon her the obvious leadership of his Church.

That Christ commissioned the Magdalene to act as Apostle to the Apostles as the first witness and leader is written in the Bible in words that brook no misinterpretation. John 20:17 *Jesus said, Do not cling to me, for I have not yet ascended to the Father. Go instead to my brothers and sisters and tell them, 'I am returning to my Father and your Father, to my God and your God'.* Clearly here, we see an important teaching from Christ to the Magdalene regarding the soul during the ascension process, which is reflected and expanded upon in the Gospel of Mary, a hugely important work that has been lost for centuries. Vatican II has at last affirmed her as Apostle to the Apostles, and as such she appears in the new *Catholic Missal*, published in 1969.

One of the most repeated mistakes represented in art and literature is the exact wording of Jesus in this encounter, another victim of the subjectivity of the translator. *'Noli me tangere'* are the words used and translated as *'Do not touch me'*. The capitalisation on the words Do not touch me, appearing in the context of art depicting the Magdalene grovelling at the feet of Jesus incline the beholder to perceive Jesus as rejecting Mary as someone who is unclean, and yet

10

this obviously cannot be, because previously in the gospels we are told that He cleansed her and restored her to health, physical and spiritual. So why then would He suddenly perceive her as unclean or unworthy, especially after her recent acceptance by Him as the one anointing Him? In a more accurate translation we see that the words recorded actually mean 'Do not cling to me' in which lays a difference in meaning. Jesus is still not in his ascended light body and is still in the process of ascension, he doesn't want Mary to think that he has returned to stay in his physical body. He is once again giving her an understanding of the state of the soul after death.

As the first to witness the resurrection she became the First Apostle and as such puts the authority of the Roman Church into question.

Elsewhere we are told that women were not only the companions of Jesus but also that they were wealthy women who financed His ministry and travelled with Him. They were obviously good enough to give their wealth to Jesus and to follow Him as disciples and yet the Roman Church still stands by their doctrine that women could not be disciples. Strange that so obviously the source of their beliefs, Jesus Christ himself, showed that the opposite was in fact true.

Pope Gregory in his homily 33 from the year 591 is the first to attribute Mary Magdalene as a prostitute as he identifies her with Luke's sinner, also with the Mary that Mark tells us had seven demons cast out of her by Christ. He then further confirms her identity as the one that anointed Jesus' feet. In this one statement he tells us that the identities of these three women are one and the same, Mary Magdalene. "We believe that this woman is Luke's female sinner, the woman John calls Mary, and that Mary from whom Mark says seven demons were cast out." He then continues to explain that she anointed Christ's feet with ointment that she had previously used "*to perfume her flesh in forbidden acts.*" Here we begin to see the perpetuation of the belief in her being a prostitute.

The confirmation that this woman is in fact Mary of Bethany comes to us directly from chapter twelve of John's gospel. "*Six days before the Passover, Jesus arrived at Bethany, where Lazarus lived, whom Jesus had raised from the dead.* (Lazarus being Mary's brother). *Here a dinner was given in Jesus' honour. Martha served, while Lazarus was among those reclining at the table with him. Then Mary took about a pint of pure nard, an expensive perfume; she poured it on Jesus' feet and wiped his feet with her hair. And the house was filled with the fragrance of the perfume.*"

This picture of the Magdalene continued right up until 1969 when the Vatican issued a statement to say that Pope Gregory had been wrong in his identification with Mary as a prostitute. A low-key statement that has had very little effect. We have all seen retractions printed in newspapers, appearing in small print on the back page. So much for Papal Infallibility. This single act does more than correct a mistake of an early pope, it is an admission that whilst the Bible in its original form was the inspired word of God, its interpretations have been subject to the uninspired decisions of men.

In this text, the original Greek word used was '*harmartolos*', translated as '*sinner*', when, in truth, it means simply one who is outside the law, and was even used to describe a person not of Jewish origin. A big leap to the designation as sinner and thence to prostitute.

So, why did this happen?

We only have to look at the history of the early church. In the beginning, women held positions of authority within the church as deaconesses and disciples, then there appears to have been a turnaround excluding women from all sacerdotal duties and orders. The Magdalene was such an important and influential figure in the Christ story that the only possible solution for the Roman Church was to present her with a bad reputation and to sully her name in order to reduce her importance in the Christ story. We have to remember that the gospels of the main canon were written almost a century after the crucifixion, Mark being the first to be written about seventy years after Christ's death; plenty of time to 'adjust' the details surrounding the Magdalene to suit the new church's structure and-policy of the exclusion of women. A policy that still has far-reaching and damaging effects today as we are only just beginning to see the ordination of women priests within the Anglican Church who continue to be excluded in the Roman Catholic establishment. Even in Anglican churches women are still not allowed to hold the position of Bishop, being allowed to progress no further than priest. As I write this, the general synod are hotly debating this issue, well, it's only taken two thousand years!

This brings us to what has become known as 'The Paul Problem'. It is no secret that Paul's letters advocate the subjugation of women, especially within the church, where they should 'keep quiet and not be permitted to teach in church' and that they are 'the possession of their husbands'. It isn't difficult to see why Paul has acquired the name 'the old bachelor'. It seems a shame that Paul, who had to vehemently defend his own position as an apostle, should by the same logic deny Mary Magdalene that status which is so obviously hers. By definition, an apostle is one who witnessed the resurrected Christ and, yes, Paul witnessed the risen Christ on the road to Damascus, but as we have seen the Magdalene was not only the first witness in the garden, she was given the specific task of taking this news to the other disciples by Christ himself. In that one act she becomes the First Apostle, the Apostle to the Apostles.

The second criteria for assuming the role of Apostle was to have been given a direct commission from Jesus himself and we see that clearly in Christ's directing her to 'go to your brothers and sisters and tell them the good news.'

Before we travel into the realms of the gospels found at Nag Hammadi we must first fully consider the evidence that lies at the heart of the New Testament. These are the documents that have come to us from direct eyewitness knowledge of the Magdalene and can be considered as historical evidence. What we also have to consider is the brevity of these references, in some cases no more than one verse; few words to convey the mere facts, behind which lie huge possibilities. Let's look at them, beginning with the first reference to Mary Magdalene, being the fact that Christ had driven seven demons from her.

Luke in chapter 8 refers to her as *Mary from whom seven demons had been cast out*. In all of the gospels we see Christ healing people and casting out demons from them, but Mary Magdalene is unique in the scriptures in the casting out of seven demons. This has led to the belief that she must have been a pretty good sinner to have accumulated that much negativity! I believe there is more to the designation of seven demons than is at first apparent.

Seven is the number of the bodily energy centres through which the spirit is channelled or travels. Known as chakras in eastern tradition, it is now widely acknowledged in spiritual and healing circles that these energy centres can become blocked, causing physical, spiritual and mental dis-ease. It is far more likely that Jesus in fact, cleansed or cleared these seven centres in Mary Magdalene thereby facilitating her healing on all levels. These energy centres have become associated with what the church has termed the Seven Deadly Sins, so if Mary was returned to health by the cleansing of these centres then it is easy to see how it could be ascribed to the removal of seven demons. The pity is, that it is for her previous unclean state that she is remembered, rather than the cleansed, purified and spiritually elevated being; her seven demons being those aspects of the self that obscure and block our spiritual vision and energy at each of those centres. In this state she was able to understand the teachings of Christ in their purest form, to see the pure truth and beauty of Christ's divinity and the density and barbarity of some of her fellow human beings. Small wonder that she threw herself in tears at his feet in gratitude, not as the penitent whore but the grateful, spiritually open disciple.

It is easy to see how this eastern mysticism was acceptable in Palestine at the time of Christ as it travelled from India to Babylon and from there into Egypt. The biblical association with Egypt is well documented and Christ himself lived in Egypt for quite a considerable time.

Also, within Gnostic mythology, there are seven levels to the cosmos, seen in the sun, the moon and the five planets. These were seen as demonic forces entrapping us in matter. Gnostic awakening from the material world was seen as a seven steps to the ogdoad (the eighth level – the firmament) Freeing Mary from her seven demons represents Jesus assisting Mary in her ascension process.

The next reference in the scriptures to look at closely is the record of her anointing Jesus' head and feet at Bethany. Mark chapter 14 describes her with an alabaster jar of very expensive perfume, made of pure nard (spikenard), which she broke and poured out over his head and feet.

Before we even get to the nard, the fact that the jar is alabaster is important. It was an extremely costly material, translucent and white, carved from a single piece of the mineral. It was used mainly in Egypt and there especially, it was used in association with funeral rites and the anointing ritual.

Matthew's gospel clearly shows us that Christ in his defence of Mary when the other disciples reprimanded her for her waste of costly oils, accepted the fact that she had anointed him for burial (Matthew 26:12) *'When she poured this perfume on my body, she prepared me for my burial'*. Here we have another reference, this time from Jesus himself, to the funerary practices of Egypt where the anointing of the bodies of the God-Kings with special oils was intended to assist the soul in its travels through seven veils to the Source. In Jewish tradition, anointing for burial had to be done by family members, so perhaps we have a hint here of a closer relationship between the two.

Judaic Law of the time forbade a woman to free and uncover her hair in front of any but her husband, as this was an outward sign of sexual license. For an unknown or unmarried woman to have done this before Christ and then proceeded to wipe his feet with her hair would have caused an outrage amongst the disciples had it not have been that she was considered to have been acting legitimately. However, the only outrage that we see in the gospel is that brought about by the use of such a costly oil.

Another canonical hint at the true relationship of the Magdalene to Christ can be found in the account of His first miracle, at the wedding in Cana when Jesus turned water into wine. Here he is treated not as an important guest but in fact as the head of the household. The servants came to him and to no-one else for direction when the wine had run out. They obeyed His instruction alone. If in fact he was the head of this household, then who was the bridegroom? Was it in fact Christ himself?

A picture is forming of Mary Magdalene as having intimate knowledge of these practices and an understanding of death and the progress of the soul after death. This is reflected in religious art as almost everywhere we find the Magdalene portrayed, we see a skull, indicating her close link to death. Christ it seems not only understood this aspect of Mary but accepted her ministrations as of necessity.

The anointing also has a deeper significance when we consider how Matthew's gospel continues, in Jesus' insistence that 'everywhere the gospel is preached, throughout the world, what she has done will also be told, in remembrance of her.' Clearly this act has impacted on Christ in a big way and it is Mary that he wants remembered in this event. One fact that cannot be denied is that the word 'Christ' is a direct translation of 'anointed one'. This anointing then, is multi purpose. The preparation for burial, the ritual anointing that will assist the soul in its journey through the underworld and something else. The designation of Jesus as 'the Christ', the 'anointed one' who was awaited by all Israel, the Messiah that had been foretold. It was Mary Magdalene alone who has recognised and acknowledged Jesus for his true identity as the Messiah and acted accordingly.

At this point it is perhaps appropriate to examine another casualty of the translator in the nard itself. The original Greek translates as 'genuine' nard. What is important here? The term genuine nard designates this as authentic anointing oil, the anointing oil of priests and kings, the anointing oil of the royal line of David. So we have Jesus anointed as King, as the anointed one or Messiah and also anointed in prepar-ation for his death. This is a huge thing to have been left in the hands of a penitent prostitute, and of course it wasn't.

Mary was obviously skilled in the death rites of the Egyptian temples, and was close enough to Jesus himself for him to wish her acknowledged for the act. No wonder he wanted her remembered for this, it was His anointing as Priest and King, as Messiah.

But what of the anointing as King? Could Mary have had the necessary authority to do this? We can find the answer in her name.

Scriptures tell us she was Mary Magdalene; other translations call her Miryam of Magdala. Whilst we have been led to believe that she was from the town of Magdala, and that was the origin of her name, archaeologists have recently pointed out that the town of Magdala did not exist at the time of Christ, or if it did, that it was known by some other name. In fact 'Magdalene' is derived from the Hebrew word *M'gdal* meaning Pillar, Tower or Watchtower. This term also referred, on a mundane level, to the watchtower from where shepherds kept watch over their flocks, and therefore it is an easy stretch to the deeper level reference to the Watchtower of the Flock of Israel, the Magdal-Eder. According to many ancient beliefs, Mary was from the tribe of Benjamin and in fact the Roman church went to the lengths of genocide in France when they murdered hundreds of Cathars at Beziers who not only believed this was the true lineage of the Magdalene but that she was also the wife or consort of the Christ. This tribe of Israel passed down the line of succession through the females and the term that was designated as one of authority was 'pillar' following their understanding that the family was a building and the pillar was the structure holding up the edifice. So Mary Magdalene, Mary the Pillar, if she was indeed heir to the tribe of Benjamin was therefore worthy of the duty of anointing Jesus as the Christ, the King, and the Messiah.

The gospels also give confirmation of this, as they describe her standing behind Jesus and pouring out the oil onto his head, which was in fact the manner adopted for the anointing of royalty.

Mary appears to have acted in the traditions of the Priestesses of Isis gifted in the assistance of the spirit through life and death and into life again. Parallels can also be drawn in this context with the gifts of Gold, Frankincense and Myrrh that were brought to the infant Jesus. Spikenard was known in the temples to ease the transition between life and death.

A further look at the anointing rituals of the middle east at that time lead us to the marriage anointing of the bridegroom/ priest-king by the bride or goddess figure, such as can be found in the rituals of Ishtar and Isis. The bridegroom destined to be sacrificed for the sake of his people is ritually anointed by his bride as part of the sacred marriage or heiros gamos. Language again provides us with a clue to the true import of these events.

Heiros Gamos became 'Holy Matrimony' which means 'sacred marriage'. The rite of the sacred marriage entailed the anointed God/King being filled with the God essence and the bride being filled with the Goddess essence prior to and during the consummation of the marriage. Clearly there are parallels with the Magdalene and Christ here and further reason for him to permit her to do the anointing. Are we really being shown by this act, the actual marriage ceremony of Jesus and Mary? Interestingly, the gospels show that the displeasure shown by the disciples, especially Judas Iscariot, at this act was directed at the cost of the unguent not the act itself. The inference has to be that they were used to witnessing the intimacy between Christ and the Magdalene. Indeed, this is clarified in the gospel of Thomas where we see Peter complain that the Lord loved her more than the others and that he often kissed her on the mouth. The fact that a woman was forbidden by Judaic Law to touch a man who was not her husband, in public, yet here was the Magdalene obviously in intimate contact with Christ and kissing him on the mouth; a pretty strong indication of the relationship between the two.

Returning to the gospels and the words of Jesus himself, we hear this story countless times in churches read from pulpits by clergy and laity alike and yet this woman remains anonymous. Christ's wishes were heeded only to a certain extent when he asks that *'wherever the gospel is preached throughout the world, what she has done will be also told, in memory of her.'* This is so obviously a matter of huge importance to Christ and has to be obeyed but surely an event of this magnitude to Him would warrant the identity of the woman to be part of the 'memory of her'. In addition, throughout the gospels, we see Jesus quick to rebuke anyone who had broken Jewish Laws, for him to then permit Mary, with her unbound hair, to touch him, anoint him and kiss him in public without censure would be a complete contradiction of his previous actions. Not only does He permit it, He defends her actions and insists that they are remembered wherever the gospel is preached throughout the world. Is He asking here, that His bride be recognised as such?

It is interesting to note that in the whole of the Bible texts we see only two rites performed on Jesus; one at the beginning of his ministry, the baptism in the River Jordan by John the Baptist and again at the end of his ministry by Mary of Bethany/Mary Magdalene. Also interesting is the fact that John the Baptist is also given small mention in these same gospels.

Further indication of the importance of the Magdalene in the Christ story is her place in many of the lists of names mentioned in the gospels as being witness to or with Christ at important times in His ministry. Her name appears at the head of lists, taking priority even over Mary the Mother of Christ. She is treated with the deference of one holding the position of first lady in the story, especially at such a crucial point as the crucifixion where Mark 15:40 tells us *'Some women were watching from a distance. Among them were Mary Magdalene, Mary mother of James the younger, Joses and Salome* (identifying this Mary as Mary the mother of Jesus).

We find another reference to Mary at the crucifixion, at the foot of the cross with Mother Mary and John. The other disciples have long since fled in fear for their own lives and are nowhere to be seen, including Peter who having denied Jesus three times compounds his shame with cowardice. It is left to those who are closest to Christ to witness the harrowing death and suffering on the cross and to be there as his broken body is removed for burial. This alone puts her into the perspective of family, as once again we turn to Judaic tradition to discover that the spouse and close family carried out the preparation of a body and the actual interment.

When we next encounter Mary within the canonical gospels it is as first witness to the resurrection. She is grief stricken and arrives at the tomb to finish the ritual anointing and preparation of Jesus' body only to find the tomb open and empty. As the risen Christ approaches her and utters her name, 'Mary', her response indicates the level of love and intimacy between the two. 'Rabboni', she whispers, her grief disappears in an instant and she addresses the Saviour in a way that we see nowhere else in the gospels. Rabbouni, the intimate form of Rabbi, not a term attributed to any other of the disciples, who address Him as Lord, Saviour or Master, clearly it is a term of endearment that is special within their relationship. He explains his physical state to her and it is not difficult to imagine that some special teaching is given during this encounter and then He tasks her to go and tell the other disciples of His resurrection, as Magdalene the First Apostle.

There can be no argument to that; it is clearly worded in the accepted or canonical gospels. Peter's religious authority within the Catholic Church and thence into the Anglican Church has stemmed from those churches acceptance of the fact that he was the first to witness the risen Christ, which seems ludicrous when even in the canonical gospels, three out of the four clearly state that it was Mary who was the first witness.

It is from this point forwards that we must look to other historical documents to get a clearer picture of the true status and role of one of the most enigmatic and misrepresented characters in the whole of the Jesus story. One question does remain, however. If Mary Magdalene was of the little importance attributed to her in the accepted scriptures, then why would the early Roman Church elevate her to sainthood? Why canonise her to Saint Mary Magdalene and afford her a special feast day along with the other disciples? The official description of Saint Mary Magdalene by the Roman Church is 'Disciple of our Lord'. Seems like a question of wanting it both ways, doesn't it? Firstly, there are no women disciples then we find Saint Mary Magdalene, Disciple of our Lord. This is simply another puzzle surrounding this woman who was described as the consort of Jesus and one who has clearly been delivered a raw deal.

Another question that has to be asked is this. If Mary Magdalene was the wife/consort of Jesus, then why was she absent from the Last Supper? In my opinion, she wasn't. I realise that I am treading perilously close to the Leonardo Da Vinci's Last Supper debate and furore but it is unavoidable if a satisfactory answer is to be found.

Logic would dictate that an event with such far reaching and profound effect on Jesus would demand her presence. And surely, she was there.

Dan Brown's *Da Vinci Code* makes reference to the Last Supper by Leonardo containing hidden symbolism and purporting the theory that it has in fact been changed. The theory is that the effeminate figure on Christ's right is not in fact John but the Magdalene. The figure in question is dressed in direct mirror of Christ, both wearing red and blue robe and cloak, reversed on the John/Magdalene figure. Art historians maintain that John was traditionally painted as effeminate but this cuts little ice with those who wonder why some artists portray John and Mary as identical or why so many copies of the famous Last Supper clearly show a female figure.

An interesting 'side-effect' of this interest in Leonardo's masterpiece is that if the figure in question is in fact Mary Magdalene, then the aggressive stance and open hostility of the figure of Peter is more easily understood.

Peter's threatening gesture towards her makes perfect sense when seen in relation to the gnostic Gospel of Phillip. It also appears to have been common debate in Leonardo's era that Mary was more than she was allowed to appear and that she had importance outside of the Orthodox Church that had effectively demoted her to a lesser character.

Another anomaly in the scriptures is the question of why, if she was indeed the wife of Jesus, was she missing at Pentecost? The Holy Spirit was given as an inspirer of the disciples, the giver of the gifts of faith and healing and as we will see during our closer look at Mary, this really wasn't her style.

Mary's strength lay in her intimate relationship with Jesus and thence with God, she needed no intermediary as she walked an inner pathway to ascension through pure and direct knowledge of the divine. Hers was a path of inner knowledge, inner working, and inner transformation, so akin to the feminine divine with which she is now associated.

Interestingly, the Eastern Orthodox Church has never subscribed to the notion that the Magdalene was a repentant sinner or whore. They place her in high regard, and in one of their texts they have her in Ephesus after the ascension of Jesus, with John and Mary, mother of Jesus, then later in Rome meeting with the Emperor Tiberius, preaching the resurrection. Tiberius is supposed to have said that a man could no more be resurrected from the dead than an egg could turn red. In response Mary picked up an egg which immediately turned red. Is this the reason why she is often depicted in art as holding an egg?

There seems to be more and more questions emerging about this enigmatic and wondrous woman. I hope that some of the answers will be found in these pages.

Chapter Two

The Magᵭalene of the Hiᵭᵭen Gospels

What are the 'hidden' gospels? More commonly known as the Gnostic gospels, these papyrus manuscripts were uncovered from the desert sands of Egypt, along the banks of the Nile, in 1945 by two farmers digging in the sand at the foot of the cliffs that fringed the river. The stone jar that they unearthed contained, not treasure as they first hoped, but something more valuable than gold itself. The documents that they had brought to light were none other than the gospels and writings that have become known as the Nag Hammadi Library in reference to the place of their discovery. Among these manuscripts were the Gospel of Thomas, The Secret Gospel of John and the Gospels of Phillip and Bartholomew. In total there were thirty three books and many other records of the early Christians. These gospels were among the many other records and manuscripts which were deliberately excluded from the canon by the Council of Nicea and which, by supreme coincidence, give a more graphic and clear picture of the importance of Mary Magdalene and indeed of her true relationship with Jesus Christ. If, like me, you believe there are no coincidences, we must ask ourselves if there is a link between their content and their exclusion. One of the most obvious differences between the canonical gospels and the hidden gospels is the nature of their content. We find in the canonical gospels the outward and overt teachings of Jesus both direct and indirect in the form of parables, records of his journeys and of his miracle working and healing. The Gnostic gospels however, take us to a completely different sphere of existence as they address the spiritual truth and messages of Christ that lead to the perfection of the human soul. The Gospel of Mary Magdalene, although scant in its survival, is perhaps the most important of all of the manuscripts found that give insight and relevance to this work and as such it has been allocated a chapter of its own.

One of these hidden gospels, the Gospel of Thomas, repeats and reinforces most of the writings that became the New Testament but it also contains information and material that completely changes the perspective of the early church and reveals teachings of Jesus that not only contradict the doctrines of the Roman Church but also provide the ground from which the Magdalene is revealed in all her glory.

The one part of this document that blows the lid on the true status of the Magdalene is also clouded by mistranslation. One aspect of the Greek language that is reassuring is that it is very specific in its meanings, there is one word for one meaning in Greek and this gives us safe ground for the interpretation of the terms used. In the Gospel of Thomas, in its original Greek, we find the word 'koinonos', which very specifically means 'consort' or 'companion of a sexual nature' here translated as simply 'companion'. The text reads as follows; *'the companion (koinonos) of the Saviour is Mary Magdalene. But Christ loved her more than all the other disciples and used to kiss her often on her mouth. The rest of the disciples were offended... they said to Him, 'Why do you love her more than all of us?' The Saviour answered them, 'Why do I love her more than all of you?'* In all of the gospels we rarely see Jesus answer a question with a question, and it is easy to 'hear' the intonation in his voice as he asks this question as being one of disbelief that the disciples don't 'get it'.

It is perhaps in this text from the Gospel of Phillip that we find the most pointed references to the Magdalene being the consort of Christ, his *'koinonos'* and the intimate union that became honoured in France.

Another of the papyri found at Nag Hammadi has become known as the Dialogue of the Saviour and it is here that we find the most direct reference to the Magdalene and her status in the eyes of Christ himself. He refers to her as a great visionary that is far above the other disciples and he calls her 'the woman who knows the All'. This gives us a direct confirmation that Jesus had singled Mary out for special teaching and advanced understanding of the nature of his spiritual message. Throughout this document we see Mary as the most prominent voice that both asks questions and understands what Jesus is really teaching.

One document that was not found in Nag Hammadi, and yet is still known as a Gnostic gospel, is the Gospel of Mary Magdalene. This was not included in the find at Nag Hammadi but was discovered earlier in Cairo in 1896 written in Coptic and in a fragmented condition. It nevertheless completes the picture of the early struggle of the Magdalene to bring the post resurrection teachings of Christ to the rest of the Apostles who had, in keeping with the traditions of the day, ignored the example set by Jesus in His respect for Mary and formed an elite group surrounding Peter as their leader and spokesman. We see in this gospel, the Apostles deep in mourning and grief for the loss of the Saviour and yet it is to the Magdalene that they turn for reassurance and ask her to reveal some of the secret teachings to them. We can see the mainstream church's description of this event in Marks gospel, when he relates, 'Now when he arose on the first day of the week, he appeared first to Mary Magdalene out of whom he had driven seven demons. She went and told those who had been with him and who were mourning and weeping. When they heard that Jesus was alive and she had seen him, they didn't believe it.'

In the Gospel of Mary Magdalene, the surviving text shows us on page nine, the moment where the Magdalene finds the apostles weeping and mourning and once again consumed with fear for their own lives. *How do we go among the unbelievers and announce the kingdom of the Son of Man? They didn't spare his life, why then should they spare ours?'* Apparently the other disciples still haven't fully achieved their own inner peace with the kingdom of the Son of Man. Mary responds to them not with tears, but with love and encouragement that stems from a deeper knowledge and understanding of the soul and its presence. She embraces them all with a tenderness for each and every one in the unconditional love that Jesus taught.

'Do not remain in sorrow and doubt, for his Grace will guide you and comfort you. Let us instead praise his greatness for he has prepared us for this. He is calling upon us to become fully human (? to fully embrace our humanity in spirit). *Thus Mary turned their hearts towards the Good, and they began to discuss the Teachers words.

Mary agrees to explain to them the teachings that she has personally received and afterwards finds that her words have fallen on deaf or defiant ears, ears that cannot and will not hear. Andrew is the first to challenge her teaching as he asks the others, *'Tell me, what do you think of these things that she has been telling us? As for me I do not believe that the Teacher would speak like this. These ideas are too different from those we have known."* A clear indication here of the two different levels of teaching that had been going on. An outwardly mundane teaching to those whose imaginations and perhaps intelligence was limited to everyday interpret-ation, and a teaching on an esoteric level designed to aid those whose seeking was on the spiritual planes.

Peter then joins the denial and criticism, and his dislike and rivalry of the Magdalene comes to the fore. *'How is it possible that the Teacher talked in this manner with a woman about secrets of which we ourselves are ignorant? Must we change our customs and listen to a woman? Did he really choose her, and prefer her to us?'* In just two sentences we see the begin-nings of the church's repression of women that has dogged our society for two millennia. Women within the church became 'less than' in that moment. Never mind that the Saviour on whose existence the church was formed clearly was in disagreement with this practice, Peter here set the tone and future doctrine that has denied humanity the true message of Christianity to this day.

Even the outward teachings of Christ, being one of love for all mankind, is flouted at this moment by Peter in his insecurity and jealousy of the woman who Jesus loved above all others, except possibly His mother, Mary, and his disbelief that the Master could possibly do such a thing.

The Magdalene is devastated at this point. Beside herself with grief for the loss of her Beloved whilst understanding its deeper significance, she tries to give comfort to the others only to be disbelieved and insulted by Peter whose anger is barely disguised. She weeps and tries to appeal to Peter, 'My brother Peter, what can you be thinking? Do you believe this is just my imagination, that I invented this vision? Or do you think I would lie about the Teacher?'

Obviously distraught that not only her entire relationship with Christ is being cast aside but that they could possibly believe that she would lie about Him. Enter Levi in her defence.

Levi scolds Peter for being hot-headed, a feature of Peter's character that we see often displayed in the gospels, and also for behaving in a way that was in keeping with what Christ had been there to change, and therefore behaving in a way directly opposed to Christ's teachings.

He says, *'Peter, you have always been hot-headed and now we see you repudiating a woman just as our adversaries do. Yet, if the Teacher held her worthy, who are you to reject her? Surely the Teacher knew her very well, for He loved her more than us.'*

It hadn't taken Peter long to return to his old belief systems and behaviours and to forget the ultimate request of Jesus, to love one another as he had loved them. He takes the role here as an adversary rather than a friend or brother

So what was it that Mary had tried to explain to them that had caused such outrage? It is clear that she is talking to them of visions that she has had of the Saviour since his death and resurrection as she relays the information she received at these times, what we would today refer to as channelling. She discusses the make-up of the soul, the mechanics of its existence and how the soul ascends. None of this makes any sense to Peter in his locked-in attitude to the physical reality of the world. His interests are vested in the return to what he sees as the rightful subordination of women to the authority of men despite Jesus' obvious example to the opposite.

What seems to have emerged from this encounter is the beginnings of the two distinct churches that are becoming more and more acknowledged, the outer church of Peter and the inner church of Mary and John; The orthodox and the Gnostic, the former dwelling on the past and the history and outward teachings of Jesus and the latter affirming the knowledge of the eternal and living Christ appearing to his disciples in visions and in his etheric body with a deep understanding of the higher teachings of Jesus.

What we can clearly see at this point in the examination of Christianity then and now, the orthodox and the Gnostic is that it is very much down to personal belief and faith. Therein lies the difference between the two concepts. Belief stems from sight or physical evidence of the subject whereas faith, whilst not blind, must be present without the need for physical evidence. 'You pays your money and you makes your choice', or so they say. With Christianity it is not so simple. We have direct evidence that Jesus of Nazareth existed and taught his way through Palestine, he was tried and crucified for sedition and we have eye witness accounts of his resurrection and ascension. We also have indirect evidence of his inner spiritual messages from recently unearthed documents, those same documents that cast doubt on his life as a celibate or sterile God.

The rituals that we have sight of in the canonical gospels and in the Gospels of Phillip and Thomas between the Magdalene and Christ have their antecedents in widespread mythology throughout the Middle East. The sacred union or heiros gamos was celebrated long before the advent of Christianity in the worship of Inanna and Damuzi, Ishtar and Tammuz, Isis and Osiris in Egypt. Common also to all of these religions is the role of the bridegroom as sacrificed for his people. Also common to all these mythologies is the reunion of the resurrected bridegroom with his beloved in a garden setting. The parallels between the Christ/Magdalene story and these others are striking if not conclusive.

In the use of parables in his teaching Jesus refers often to the Bridegroom and shows himself in that role. Rome is quick to assert that it was allegory for Christ being the Bridegroom and the church as his Bride. He also refers to himself as the 'Shepherd or the Good Shepherd', on a mundane level this could have been used in order to reach the people's understanding, being rural people for the most part, familiar with the world of the shepherd and his responsibilities. These points parallel perfectly with the Damuzi/Tammuz mythos whereby both of these deities were known as Shepherd Kings and also the sacrificed Bridegroom killed for the sake of their people to be buried and rise again in perpetuation of the fertility rites and practices of their followers.

Margaret Starbird in her *Woman with the Alabaster Jar* shows terrific insight when she compares the Jesus/ Magdalene scenario to the ancient Song of Songs, as have many other Magdalene writers. At first glance it could easily be a case of making the evidence fit the desired response but this ancient canticle is so obviously about the sacrificed Bridegroom and the parallels truly are there for all to see when looked at with the most dispassionate eyes. The Song of Songs is quite clearly about the Sacrificed Bridegroom which served as part of the anointing ritual of old and as performed by the Magdalene on Jesus during the Sacred Marriage ceremony.

As Margaret Starbird points out, the Song of Songs was accepted by the Jewish rabbis as part of their tradition and also very popular at the time of Jesus. His disciples would have been familiar with it and its deeper meanings. Why then was the only protest at the anointing made by the disciples on the grounds of the cost of the oil itself and not the meaning of her actions? It also reiterates their familiarity with the intimacy between Jesus and Mary that they don't protest at her touching Jesus but only with what they perceive as waste. Of all of these religions that may have influenced Christ it is likely to be the Isis/Osiris union of his early years. So too, do we see traces of the temples of Isis in the acts of the Magdalene. Several authors have postulated on the fact the Mary was a priestess of Isis and that her reputation as a prostitute stems from the fact she was an initiate of the secrets of Isis based on sex magic and sexual alchemy. It is well within the bounds of possibility that this was so, although there is no direct evidence for this, certainly the worship of Inanna and Isis were commonplace in Judea at the time of Christ and certainly there was a large Jewish population in Alexandria in Egypt at that time too. The blending of beliefs and practices was more than likely.

Whatever her initial beliefs or training, one thing becomes increasingly apparent and that is that the Magdalene became the most intimate companion of Jesus and was the one to perpetuate his teachings on a higher level.

One thing that is striking about the Jesus story is its appearance as prophesies in the Old Testament. The prophets Isaiah, Micah and the Psalms of David all tell of the messiah to come, the holy Christ that will lead the children of Israel to freedom. Christ himself tells us that he has come not to abolish the old laws but to fulfil them by fulfilling the prophecies.

Small wonder then, that the zealots among his followers were expecting him to lead them in bloody battle back to the throne of Israel, or at their disappointment when their messiah's message was a spiritual one of love, tolerance and reconciliation, not only for the Jews but the Gentiles alike. It was a surprise to Jesus also to realise that his mission was to include all nations and all people as we can so clearly see when he heals the Canaanite woman and realises then that he has been sent for the sake of all mankind and not just to deliver the Jews from Roman oppression. It is perhaps at this moment of realisation that another possibility comes to the fore.

If the Jews were to return a King to the throne of David then a marriage between two powerful tribes such as Benjamin (The Magdalene) and Judah, through the House of David, (Jesus) would almost certainly guarantee its success. If the people of Israel were looking for a warrior king to restore the throne to them then their lessons were certainly harsh ones but it would certainly explain their acceptance of the Magdalene's presence amongst them, however much they disagreed with her later.

If the Magdalene was the wife or consort of Jesus, why then was she absent from the Last Supper, an event that clearly held much significance for Jesus and for the continuation of his ministry. As we have seen, she wasn't and if nothing else, logic would determine that she would indeed have been present. Whilst I cannot comment on the truth behind the claims that Leonardo disguised the figure of the Magdalene as a man, it does seem strange that the figure pictured in this work of art is remarkably feminine, even to the hint of breasts, and also that the clothing on Jesus and this enigmatic figure are an exact reversal of each other.

Chapter Three

The Magdalene Trail

I had expected to begin the journey in France, near Marseilles on the south coast of Provence, and work my way back up through the country tracing The Magdalene's presence through her shrines and churches dedicated to her. But the best laid plans of mice and men they say...

It was whilst I was looking into a trip to Scotland to visit the now famous Rosslyn Chapel, thanks to the *Da Vinci Code*, that I came across some information that would lead me to something wonderful. My joyous and loud shout of 'Yes!' as I looked at the picture that has become the front cover of this book made the entire house come see what was the matter!

The Magdalene it seemed had been in Scotland. In his brilliant book *The Holy Land of Scotland*, author and historian Barry Dunford brought my attention to the beautiful little Kilmore Church on the highland Isle of Mull and the wonderful stained glass window illustrating what appeared to be Jesus cradling a very pregnant Mary Magdalene in his arms, so powerful was the image that it had to be the cover of this book.

Like Barry, my first thought was that if indeed this wasn't Christ and his beloved Magdalene then who was it? If, as has been maintained by the established church, the window represented Joseph and Mother Mary then indeed it was strange to see the halo depicted around Joseph's head and not Mary's, she being the holy one and not he. In any case, the inscription in the window defies misinterpretation as it clearly refers to the incident where Martha complains that Mary is not helping with the domestic chores, Instead she is sitting at the feet of Jesus as his student. The inscription on the window reads 'Mary has chosen the better part'.

I needed to see it for myself.

It had been raining all the previous day and night and on a very wet and misty morning we caught the ferry from Oban over to the Isle of Mull. Geography hadn't been my strong point, in school or afterwards, and my idea of the Isle of Mull, even though I had seen the map, was of a tiny barren island just off the west coast. I was amazed at its beauty in the first instance and then by its size. It was a good hour's drive from the ferry dock to the little village of Dervaig where it was easy to find the beautiful little Kilmore (Kilmore derives from the words 'Kil' meaning Church and Mor from Mary) Church. Set up off the road and framed by pretty trees the little white church beckoned us inside.

The entire set of stained glass windows were beautiful but the one I searched for nestled halfway down the right hand side. As I stood there in awe of the implications of what I was

MARY·HATH·CHOSEN·THAT·GOOD·PART·WHICH
SHALL·NOT·BE·TAKEN·AWAY·FROM·HER

Erected to the Glory of God. In loving memory of
Mary Forrest, of Arden. Died 29th October 1931,
by a nephew. ... the sister Isabella D Forrest ...

looking at the sun chose that moment to shine directly through the window and light up the whole scene. The colours were breathtaking, especially the blue/green of the Magdalene's robes, a colour which has become known among the faithful as 'Magdalene Blue', now seen reflected in the chrysocolla and lapis lazuli stones in the Magdalene Rosary. The inscription referencing the picture to Mary Magdalene and Christ was neatly framed central to and directly underneath the artwork. There could be no mistake.

There was an indescribable peace inside that small church that seemed to come from the window as if in acknowledgement that even in a small, out of the way church on a remote island, Jesus and His Bride were being recognised at last.

The window dates back to 1905 and was commissioned by a Thomas Eversfield. There is a plaque inside the church in memory of Thomas and it bears the Templar Cross. Is this the link between the image on the window and the Knights Templar; evidence of the true nature of the Holy Grail said to be in the keeping of the Knights of the Grail?

We strolled down the central isle of the little church and there above the altar was another piece to the puzzle. The interlocking triangles of the Star of David, a very Jewish symbol to be found inside a Christian church on a Scottish island. The answer was simple, the two triangles superimposed over each other represent of course the union of the male and female.

I could have stayed inside the church looking at the window for an age but we were headed for the Isle of Iona next, where The Akashic records of Thoth tells us that the Magdalene gave birth to a son John Martinus, conceived after Christ's resurrection by His light body, and who she left in the care of the Ionian Priestesses. This was obviously another place that deserved a visit on the Magdalene Trail.

The unsettled weather meant that it was uncertain if the Iona Ferry would be running that day. It was another hour's drive around the coastline of the island to reach the Ferry Terminal and so I had to tear myself away from this haven of peace.

Outside the little church and looking at it from a different angle we could plainly see the design, with its rounded tower, was a perfect example of the masculine and feminine in union. Even if the Iona Ferry wasn't running, I had seen enough to make the whole journey worthwhile. The Sacred Union was here for all to see, and so very close to the holy isle of Iona, Mary must surely have passed this way on her journey to that sacred island. This appeared to me to be the most reasonable explanation for the appearance of her as a revered wife of Jesus on the church window in such an out of the way place.

The news from the Ferry Terminal was that whilst the boat may be leaving for Iona, there was no guarantee of its return due to the squalls in the small channel. With a return Ferry from Mull to Oban on the mainland booked and little or no accommodation to be had on Iona it was a dicey call to make but we both knew that we had to at least set foot onto the holy island.

The captain of the ferry couldn't give us a guarantee that we would be able to return to Mull that day, all he could give us was a stoic 'maybe'. We took a chance.

The Isle of Iona is tiny and completely visible from the ferry dock on Mull, I almost felt as if a strong swimmer could make it, but our little boat pitched and tossed on the currents and waves and I quickly reversed that opinion. I wondered if the weather had been kinder to Mary on her visit to the island.

From about the halfway point, the mist and clouds lifted a little and the Abbey could be clearly seen on the headland. I knew we had made the right decision, even if we were to be stranded on Iona overnight. Whilst we were quiet, almost in meditation, the captain of the ferry came and found us. He said if we were sure to be back on the dock just half an hour after arriving on Iona, he could guarantee our return that day. Much relieved but a little disappointed at such a time limit we thanked him and set our watches!

As we walked onto the dock the rain stopped almost as if it had been switched off by some unseen hand and the sun struggled to put in an appearance although the wind still whipped at us. Normally a fair weather explorer, I didn't care, I needed to be on the island.

Barry Dunford has written some brilliant papers on the Holy Land of Scotland and in *Iona: Sacred Isle of the West* he tells us that, geologically, Iona's ancient rock strata is among the oldest on this beautiful planet, dating back 1500 million years carrying within itself a primeval and creative energy. From the moment you set foot on Iona, it can be felt. And something else: The Goddess, the Feminine Divine, The Magdalene essence seeps into your very pores. This truly is a Holy Isle. From somewhere deep in the psyche of the soul there is an unmistakable presence; a sacred presence.

Unprepared for this influx of high frequency and yet at the same time, soft, energy, I felt tears in my eyes. To be in search of The Magdalene and not to experience Iona is something I couldn't now contemplate. Thank you Barry, for leading us to this wonderful place.

With only half and hour to spend on Iona, it was obvious that the five to ten minute walk to the ruined Mary Chapel behind the Abbey would take up most of the time, we set about making a short walk inland. In good time we came to what had once been the Mary Chapel. There was no other living soul in sight and the wind had calmed to a strong breeze, so we headed into the ruins into what looked to have been the chancel of the original chapel. I can't describe the serenity that still flowed from the stone in the ruined walls. With eyes closed I could almost hear the devotional chanting of the nuns from so long ago as they sang of the Christ and of Mary.

The minutes passed quickly whilst we sat in meditation in the old Mary Chapel, where we both received some powerful insights into our journey with The Christ and The Magdalene, and we were content to return to the dock knowing that The Magdalene herself had somehow touched us and that we would return to Iona someday. I hope it's someday soon.

In the same paper by Barry Dunford, we find reference to an essay by William Sharp, writing as Fiona McLeod, about Iona. He says ' When I think of Iona I think often, too, of a prophecy once connected with Iona ... the old prophecy that Christ shall come again upon Iona, and of that later and obscure prophecy which foretells, now as the Bride of Christ, now as the Daughter of God, now as the Divine Spirit embodied through mortal birth in a Woman, as once through mortal birth in a man, the coming of a new Presence and Power: and dream that this may be upon Iona, so that the little Gaelic island may become as the little Syrian Bethlehem ... the Shepherdess shall call us home. A young Hebridean priest once told me how, 'as our forefathers and elders believed and still believe, that Holy Spirit shall come again which was mortally born among us as the Son of God, but, then, shall be the Daughter of God. The Divine Spirit shall come again as a Woman. Then for the first time, the world shall know peace'.

Clearly this is a reference to the Sacred Union of the Divine, which must take place both externally and internally to restore balance and harmony to this troubled world of ours. The Magdalene has set her course for her return; we must welcome her. Certainly, if the new coming of the Christ as a woman was to be anywhere, I could imagine no more fitting a place for the Divine Birth.

Barry Dunford shows us that another version of the Grail myth by Robert de Boron, we find Jesus talking to Joseph of Arimathea whilst in prison. Jesus purportedly says to Joseph, 'The enemy, who does nothing to save, lies in wait for them to incite them to evil, first seduced Eve because she was weaker in spirit than man; and because all mankind was reduced to captivity by a woman, God desired that all should be freed by a woman.' Perhaps Christ will come again in the body of a woman. But it is certainly very clear that the feminine aspect of humanity and divinity must have an important role in the awakening of our souls to the higher planes of existence which we have come to know as the Kingdom of heaven.

In meditation, Spirit has said that the new Christ will be born twice. Firstly born in Spirit as a dove descending from the heavens to seed the Presence on the planet, and later, born in flesh to bring about the New Kingdom of Heaven on Earth. *Then I saw a new heaven and a new earth, for the first heaven and the first earth had passed away ... I saw the new city of Jerusalem coming down out of heaven from God prepared as a Bride beautifully dressed for her husband. And I heard a loud voice from the throne saying 'Now the dwelling of God is with men.'* - Revelations 21:1-3

As we left Iona, I looked back through the fine drizzle that had begun falling like a veil of lost tears, and I believed that I left the island with a better understanding of God.

From the beautiful Islands of Mull and Iona we travelled east across Scotland to pay a visit to the Rosslyn Chapel with its historical links to the Templar Knights and therefore to the Magdalene, taking a detour northwards on the way to visit St Mary's Church in Grandtully.

There are countless Mary Chapels and churches dedicated to Mary across Scotland, interestingly most form an alignment from one side of Scotland to the other, ending on Iona, and

Kilmore Church, Isle of Mull

there can be no doubt that Marian worship was entrenched here, 'Mary' had indeed blazed a trail. But was it Mary Magdalene or was it Mary, Mother of Jesus?

St Mary's Church Grandtully looked more like a lime-washed farmhouse from the 16th Century. It was fairly remote and clearly no longer in use. Why would such an isolated building be preserved and cherished unused for so long? The answer lay inside. I had expected darkness and cold but was greeted by the automatic switching on of a light and a blast of warm air from electric fan heaters high on the walls. Instantly I was aware of the round barrelled ceiling adorned with ancient paintings that, although faded, were still in marvellous condition.

Closer inspection answered my question about such intense preservation. The symbolism which openly lay in the paintings was something I had never seen in a church before. Grail imagery was abundant, especially in the circular picture of what can only be a Grail Knight carrying a chalice in his left hand. More Templar and Grail connections appear in the Judgement tarot card, two pregnant angels, and a unicorn. The final clue is in the commissioning of the painting by Sir William Stewart, as the Stewarts have long made claim to descent from the Davidic line and the Merovingians.

When the Knights Templar came into being, under the auspices of Bernard of Clairvaux (later to be Saint Bernard of Clairvaux), the strict rules required them all to '*make obedience to Bethany and the house of Mary and Martha*'. With it clearly established that the Knights revered the Magdalene and her family, it is easy to see why so many scholars are now of the opinion that the grand and beautiful Notre Dame Cathedrals built by the Templars were not dedicated to Mother Mary as was first supposed, but to 'Our Lady' Mary Magdalene and her son.

Remains of the nunnery, Mary Chapel, Iona

The little village of Rosslyn is steeped in energy. Ley lines converge at the high alter in the Rosslyn Chapel and the effects are palpable. So palpable in fact, that the energy kept us awake all night! We discovered in the morning, that the ley ran directly from the high altar from the chapel directly through our bedroom in the beautiful guest-house behind the chapel. Good vibrations!

My first sight of the Rosslyn chapel was disappointing. I wasn't prepared for the proliferation of unsightly scaffolding. Having seen earlier photographs of its fantastic architecture, with its towers, turrets and buttresses, it took several minutes to bring its real glory into focus. Once inside however, the magic of Rosslyn took over.

No-one could deny the aura of mystique that seeped from every stone and piece of stained glass. Truly this was sacred ground. It was early in the day and there were just a handful of visitors beside ourselves, so we were able to wander and wonder to our heart's content.

Rosslyn is often referred to as The Chapel of the Grail or the Bible in stone. Certainly the carved imagery is eclectic to say the least, ranging from the Pagan symbolism of the Green Man, to Templar, Rosicrucian and Freemasonry images and of course Gnosticism. In fact the entire Rosslyn Chapel is an encoded architectural record of Gnostic faith and lore. I believe, for the true impact of Rosslyn to be acknowledged, we need to examine the climate which pervaded these islands at the time of its construction.

Repression had grown through the Inquisition, resulting in heretics, as defined by The Church, being burned at the stake. Throughout its rampage through history, The Church wielded its power like a veritable sword, damning all who did not conform to its laws which were instigated by man and not God. Their power was absolute and showed little sign of the

The Grail Knight, ceiling painting at St Mary's Chūrch, Grandtully.

laws of Christ which centred around compassion and love, tolerance and understanding. This was the atmosphere of persecution and damnation during which Earl William Saint Claire ordered the construction of Rosslyn Chapel, a guide book to Gnosis which could not be burned, a permanent standing record of the secrets of the Grail and other Gnostic revelations.

In its efforts to erase all spirituality that had nothing to do with its dogma and doctrines it declared all else as heresy. St Augustine, who incidentally described women as 'vessels of excrement' defined heresy as 'the distortion of a revealed truth by a believer or non-believer', and what is the source of such 'revealed truth'? The Church of course.

So, it is amongst heresy and persecution the Rosslyn began its sojourn into history. In a world where The Church excluded and erased all other forms of spirituality, sometimes at the price of death, and became fearful of the truth tainting their power or putting a dent in their armour of control over the masses. Education was restricted to the clergy, a good move if the only truth that is allowed to be broadcast, is the truth that suits the seats of power. In particular, knowledge of the Spirit, of personal pathways to God, such as Gnosticism, was feared, but gradually the power of the Spirit began to take hold even within the sacred vaults of Holy Mother Church.

Celtic monks were known for their spiritual purity and simplicity, finding no need for extravagant and garish clothing for their priesthood, nor the constant demand for money that pervaded The Church. The simplicity of the Celtic priests tempered with their humility became a direct challenge to the pomp and circumstance of the power base of The Church, which in reality was a far cry from the teachings of the carpenter from Galilee.

Rome's only option was to send in the troops as it were, to begin a centuries-long battle between the Celtic Church and the Roman Catholic Church. A battle that has never been really won and in fact now appears to be going in favour of the mysticism of the Celts. It can only be a gift from God that during this time of repression, persecution and execution that some of the most notable and powerful mystics and deeply spiritual men and women were born onto this earth.

What then is the significance of Rosslyn in connection with the Magdalene? The answer lies once again in her connection to the Grail. Rosslyn Chapel itself was created as a beautiful carved reliquary or resting place of the Grail. Not the cup of the carpenter, nor the bones of our precious Magdalene, but of the Grail in its representation of the path to enlightenment and to the very feet of God. The Knights Templar of course had their connection to Mary and they too had their influence on Rosslyn with their hidden room underneath the chapel where they are said to have conducted their rights of initiation.

Much of the imagery inside the Rosslyn chapel is Templar or Grail connected and not overtly connected to the Magdalene, in contrast to the church at Rennes-Le-Chateau with its magnificent statue of the Magdalene and her carvings on the main altar. To pursue this further, we must detour from the overt Magdalene Trail into the winding secret trail of the Grail quest and the possible connection between the Grail and the Magdalene which will be explored in the later chapter– Templars, Grail and Heresies.

Before we leave Britain's contribution to the Magdalene Trail we must pay a visit to the West Country, to Glastonbury Abbey, where its ancient Mary Chapel was built around 63 AD by Joseph of Arimathea. Many legends abound of Joseph travelling with Mary in Britain, one of which details Joseph being told by the Angel Gabriel to build a chapel in the honour of Mary on this site. There are further remains of another Magdalene Chapel in Glastonbury, on the western edge of the town on Bride's Mound. In Chalice Well Gardens, another link to the Grail Legend, is a small drinking fountain with a lions head, said to depict the Lion of Judah and the sacred bloodline of the Holy Grail.

Lastly, before leaving Glastonbury Abbey, on the outside wall, is a remarkable ancient inscription in the stone. It simply reads Jesus Maria. Is this a reminder of the most sacred marriage in our history? Joan of Arc carried a banner into the Crusades bearing exactly these words and legend has it that it referred to the wedding at Cana and the Grail bloodline. Just outside the Mary Chapel, are the graves of King Arthur and Guinevere, a continuation of the sacred marriage theme.

The abbey was built on the site of the original small wattle church dedicated to St Mary. This church was built in the year AD63, the year that the Magdalene died in the St Baume region of Provence and is believed to be the first church built in England.

There is yet another Mary Chapel in Glastonbury, under the guise now of the Catholic Church 'Our Lady St Mary of Glastonbury'. How do we know that it was originally dedicated to 'our' Mary and the not the mother of Jesus? Because it is in Magdalene Street.

The connections with the Magdalene in Britain are many and certainly the idea is not new. If we look to the *Song Of Jerusalem* by William Blake we can see that the Magdalene's union with Christ was certainly a concept that had roots here long ago.

'She walks upon our meadows green
The Lamb of God walks by her side

And (in) every English child is seen
Children of Jesus and His Bride.

* * * *

Across the channel we travel to the south, close to Marseilles, to the Aix au Provence region. It is said that the Magdalene landed here after her flight from the Holy Land through Egypt after the crucifixion of her Beloved, accompanied by Joseph of Arimathea and others. She preached the gospel and the teachings of Jesus and became beloved of all of the people of that area. Even today on the 25th May each year, the people process through the town from the sea, carrying her statue in remembrance of her arrival. Legend tells that the Magdalene ended her days in caves close by in St Baume and that she was fed Holy Communion daily by angels visiting her. As her death approached they carried her to the Church in St Maximim where now stands a basilica to our Magdalene. It is far more likely that she continued her preaching throughout France and the rest of Europe; passing on the teachings of her Beloved, perhaps after retreat and meditation within those caves. Whilst this part of the Magdalene's story is treated as false by many historians, clearly, when speaking with the local people of this region, the truth stands clear. St Mary Magdalene is, to them, the Goddess of Christianity. They tell of the Magdalene being driven by the authorities from Palestine as her preaching became dangerous to them, gaining credence and the following of many early Christians. According to their traditions, Mary was put out to sea with Lazarus and Martha, in a boat without sails or oars, which has the resonance of execution and not banishment. Eventually, the little boat fetched up on the shores of Provence at a place now known as Saintes Marie de la Mer, Saint Mary of the Sea, not far from Aix au Provence.

When Mary was close to death in the cave at St Baume, Mary's body was taken to the 14th century basilica at St Maximin under the direction of Pope Boniface the eighth, where to this day her relics are to be found within its sanctified walls, her skull held by a reliquary made of bronze angels and some of her remains within a sarcophagus.

The day that we visited the grotto was warm and sunny following several days of rain, as if the Magdalene herself lit our way. The grotto is in the mountains of St Baume and to get there on foot is in itself a pilgrimage. We left the car at the end of the winding mountain road and began a climb up to the grotto which took almost an hour, even though this was supposedly the easier of the two paths. Those fitter than myself can probably do it in around forty minutes! The effort was worth it. Certainly her presence is palpable in the grotto which is now preserved and occupied by nuns who hold daily services in her memory. Once inside the grotto, the doors are closed and all natural light disappears. Hundreds of candles surround the statues and shrine to the Magdalene and earthly cares disappear with the daylight. This is truly a holy place and the presence of the divine can be felt in every inch and the presence of the Magdalene falls upon each visitor with her own brand of peace.

Later, some of the Magdalene's remains were taken to Vezelay and the church there dedicated to her name. The 13th century document *Legenda Aurea* by Jacopo di Voragine (translation and story by Leonhard Kuppers et al. 1964) gives us an insight into the works of Magdalene and the relationship of the Bishop Maximinus who gave his name to the basilica of St Maximin.

'*When our Lord ascended to heaven...........and the other disciples had been expelled from Judea, the disciples went to many lands in order to spread the word of God. With these disciples was Maximinus, one of the Lord's seventy two disciples to whose guardianship had been commended Mary Magdalene. When the disciples were scattered, St Maximinus, Mary Magdalene, her brother Lazarus, her sister Martha* (another reference to our Mary Magdalene and Mary of Bethany being one and the same) ....*By God's providence they arrived in Massilia* (Marseilles).

Here we find corroboration that St Maximin had guardianship of the Magdalene and it is therefore quite understandable that on her death (legend tells us that on her approaching death, Mary was transported by angels to St Maximin, who had become Bishop of Aix, where she received the last rights and died in Maximin's arms), he would take her remains to a holy sanctuary and give his name to it.

Further into the Legenda Aurea we find the history of how Mary's remains were transported to Vezelay.

'........... *there was, in Burgundy, a duke called Gerhard..............When he founded the monastery of Vezelay he and the abbot sent a monk with a worthy following to Aix and commissioned him to bring the remains of St Mary Magdalene to Vezelay. The monk found that Aix had been completely destroyed by the heathen, but found a tomb hewn from marble and a tombstone which told of St Mary Magdalene being buried there, and in fact her story was carved into the stone. When night came, he opened the grave, took the remains and brought them to the place where he stayed. And it was then that Mary Magdalene appeared to him and told him not to be afraid but to finish the work that he had begun. The monk started for home but one mile before he could reach the monastery it seemed that the remains became so heavy that he could no longer carry them. Then the abbot with the monks from the monastery appeared in solemn procession and they all took St Mary Magdalene's remains to their domicile with the greatest of honours.'*

Numerous miracles associated with the basilica have been attributed to the Magdalene.

Chapter Four

Templars, Grail and Heresies

Current and past literature and today's film media have made a leap of faith almost, in their portrayal of the Holy Grail not as the cup of Christ which caught His blood at the crucifixion, but as the literal vessel which bore His bloodline. Certainly in many ancient cultures the symbolism of the cup as the womb and wine as the blood resonate with the chalice or the grail, and indeed the grail legends and the Knights Templar are inextricably linked. Mary Magdalene is the patron saint of the Knights Templar and appears once again in France, in the context of the Templars, in the Church of Mary Magdalene at the enigmatic hilltop village of Rennes-Le-Chateau where she is portrayed prominently and abundantly, holding the Cross and the Grail.

So, what exactly is the Grail and what are its origins? Most folk associate it with the chalice sought by King Arthur's Knights, finding it firmly embedded in the literature and music of those times, making its way into far-reaching legend. In recent times it has been designated as the cup that Jesus used at the Last Supper, when he instituted the Eucharist or Holy Communion. It was said to have been filled with his blood at the crucifixion by Joseph of Arimathea, and believed to have the powers of healing, knowledge and abundance.

To find the origin of the Grail we must look much further back in time and look once again at the origin of the word and its subsequent translations, mistranslations and misinterpretations.

Most scholars agree that the origin of the term 'Grail' has come down from the word graal, which in its own transition appears to have originated as the Sangraal or Sangreal, which in its turn derived from Sang Real or Blood Royal. The cup or vessel of the Blood Royal, in other words the Davidic bloodline, is surely an allegory for the womb of the Magdalene, the vessel that carried the true royal bloodline.

If we can sidestep here a moment, it is interesting to note the continual references within the scriptures, the gnostic gospels and also in legend, to wine which comes from the fruit of the vine. Reference is made within the Bible to the true descendants of Israel as the vine, Jesus said, I am the true vine, and in Isaiah chapter five we find the tribe of Judah, and therefore Jesus, described as a vine, the cherished plant of the Lord. Small wonder then, that in artistic interpretation of the grail, we see chalices filled with grapes, the fruit of the vine, a direct reference to bloodlines and the vessel that carries the line. It isn't therefore, a huge leap, to associate the vine with the Messianic bloodline.

It would make perfect sense, that the bloodline of the vine be protected, and throughout legend and history we find guardians of the grail or custodians of the secret. The Templars were the most prominent of these, dedicated not only to the Lady but to the protection of the grail. This being so, then it was Jesus' duty to continue the Davidic line through marriage and children.

Our travels along the Magdalene Trail, as we now called it, took us into the heart of France, into Grail country and into the realm of the Sacred Feminine once again.

Rennes-Le-Chateau, which interestingly enough translates as Queen of the House (of David?) has become a treasure hunter's paradise since the publication of several books in which the Abbe Berangers Sauniere, a priest of the 1880's, is purported to have discovered a hidden treasure in the church. Certainly he became a very wealthy man following his said discovery of ancient manuscripts. But what exactly did he discover? And what was the exact nature of this treasure? Some claim that it was the lost treasure of the Knights Templar, some say it was secret information with which Sauniere proceeded to blackmail the church. Whatever it was, the secret went with him and we are just left to wonder. It is a strange fact though, that on his deathbed, Sauniere made a confession to another priest who was so shocked he refused absolution and last rites.

Whatever else went on at Rennes-Le-Chateau, it became an important base of the Magdalene followers and the church dedicated to her. As in the Provence region, where hundreds of shrines sprang up in her name, the Magdalene was firmly entrenched in the spiritual daily practices.

This is the hot topic of debate in many schools of thought not the least of which are those who believe that Mary Magdalene was indeed the Holy Grail and the bearer of Christ's bloodline.

Statue in St Mary's Church, Rennes-Le-Chateau

Approaching Rennes-Le-Chateau from the plain below, through the town of Couiza, we were immediately drawn into a sense of mystery and awe at the raised plateau that brought to mind images of Conan Doyle's *Lost World*. Whilst not surrounded by impenetrable jungle this plateau was equally imbued with its own aura of somewhere lost in time. Henry Lincoln describes it as *'une ville perdue – a lost city'*. The first glimpse of the mystery is the battlements of the Magdala Tower, built as a library by Sauniere, the impoverished and humble priest turned very wealthy man.

As we were visiting Rennes-Le-Chateau from the perspective of the Magdalene and not the hoards of treasure hunters we headed immediately for the church named for her. Right above the entrance to the church is a statue depicting her carrying the cross and the grail, inviting us inside.

At first, it seemed as though everything inside had been gilded and made garish in comparison to the rest of the place, strange, until we recall that it was created this way by Sauniere, it was his way of making a statement. The Magdalene was the treasure.

In the midst of all the intrigue and speculation there has to be a significance in the dedication of this little church to Mary Magdalene. In my view it simply acts as an indicator that the real treasure, the real mystery surrounding Rennes-Le-Chateau is of religious or mystical importance.

The altar inside the church depicts Mary Magdalene, in bas relief, kneeling at the entrance to a cave, a reference to her living in the grotto of St. Baume and we are told that Sauniere himself was responsible for the painting of it.

All around Rennes Le Chateau we find constant and abundant reference to Mary Magdalene; the statue outside the church, the statue inside and the beautiful altar itself.

Statue of Mary Magdalene
on top of the pillar in which
Berangere Sauniere was
supposed to have found the
treasure.

The church is named for her and a house built by Sauniere was named Villa Bethania or 'House of Bethany', the extravagant and wonderful Tour Magdala that Sauniere created to house his library. Magdalene, Magdalene everywhere. Awesome. Something fleeting popped into my mind here. I once read that the best place to hide something is where it can be seen by everyone. That is certainly true of Rennes. While the frenzied treasure hunters seek out gold, the real treasure is on display for all to see, the treasure of the Sacred Feminine.

Rennes Le Chateau, it seems, is a perfect example of sacred geometry. I groaned aloud. Mathematics in any guise, has never been my strong point, in fact I have remained comfortable in the knowledge that I am 'left brained' and thus destined for a life whereby the mysteries of mathematics has given way to a love of language. Yet, here, in the middle of my search, I am faced with this geometric design on the landscape that is purported to prove a link to the planet Venus and thus to Mary, our Magdalene. I will make the best and simplest interpretation of it that I can, in the hope that what is obviously an important aspect of the Magdalene Trail may shed further light onto her status.

In essence, the theory of sacred geometry in relation to Rennes is that of the pentagram or five pointed star which is the symbol for Venus, traced on the landscape of the Languedoc region with Rennes Le Chateau resting at one of the points. As above, so below, or, on earth as it is in heaven.

Point A = Bezu summit – also known as Templar ruins
Point B = High Mountain peak which is also aligned with Templar Ruins
Point c = The Tour Magdala at Rennes Le Chateau
Point D = Blanchefort – ancient watchtower
Point E = Mountain peak of La Soulane

The Magdalene Tower built by Sauniere

The Venus Transit forms a Pentagram in the night sky as the planet travel through the heavens and as the Magdalene is associated with Venus, we can't ignore the connection, however tenuous reflected on the landscape of a region steeped in Magdalene worship.

In his book *The Key to the Sacred Pattern*, Henri Lincoln says,

"As they turn, the planets are showing us the mysterious workings of God's hand, expressed in the harmonious movements of the spheres... each planet, as it revolves in its orbit, reaches positions where Earth, Sun and Planet form distinct alignment patterns... only one planet shows us a perfect geometrical form. This form is pentagonal and the planet is Venus. Creating five equally-spaced alignments over a period of eight years, she draws the perfect, hidden and secret symbol of the five-pointed star in the heavens... as above, so below. The very landscape bears the sign of her secret revelation."

This eight year pentagonal transit began in 2004 and ends in 2012. This is the date being bandied around by those that subscribe to the end of days scenario, the return of the Goddess and mass ascension being in 2012, or at the very least a mass spiritual awakening to the sacred feminine. The Cosmic Mother is making herself known at the beginning of the end of time as we know it.

Whilst Rennes Le Chateau provides us with a link to the Templars it isn't conclusive and so I returned to the earlier grail legends and the formation of the Templars who also became known as the Grail Knights.

In 1099 the city of Jerusalem fell to the Crusaders when the Saracen army was defeated and Godfroi of Lorraine, who by 'coincidence', was of the Davidian line and also of the Merovingian line, was given the title of Defender of the Holy

Sepulchre. In the Crusader's eyes, the House of David was returned to the throne in Jerusalem. Here began the grail legends and all of Europe became ablaze with tales of the Crusades, of Godfroi, and of 'Our Lady'.

Down throughout the twists and turns of history to the twelfth century, the Provence area of southern France maintained its devotion to the Sacred Feminine, whether or not under the guise of the Magdalene openly or underground, whilst the rest of Europe succumbed to the misogynistic teachings of St Augustine and denied value of any description to women, thereby perpetuating the Catholic Church's patriarchy. Provence was the only remaining exception to this pattern, and during the twelfth century the women of this area were held in high regard, eventually giving rise to Eleanor of Acquitaine and contrary to the belief that it was the Crusades that began this awakening in the twelfth century, the area had been the centre of Mary Magdalene worship throughout. The Crusades, however, did give rise to the Knights Templar with their devotion to 'Our Lady', and many of their number came from the noble houses of Provence.

Research into Grail legend and 'heresy' isn't complete without a close look at the Albigensian crusades and the Cathars. 'Albigensian' stems from the town of Albi where, in 1165, the Church sent a delegation to discuss and issue edicts against those they deemed heretics, principally the Cathars, though all who were deemed guilty of heresy of any nature subsequently became known as Albigensians.

Margaret Starbird has an interesting slant on the result of the Albigensian Crusades, with her reference to the Troubadours, the wandering minstrels, singers and songwriters who performed romantic songs in honour of 'The Lady', the woman that they would give their all to serve, who was beautiful, and was the embodiment of love. Whilst this in itself strikes a chord with the adherents to the Magdalene, it goes further in its identity of her as 'The Lady'. The troubadours called their 'Lady', the Dompna, which has its root in the word Domina, the Latin for Lady with Dominus as Lord, a term frequently used for Jesus.

It was for the Dompna that many a knight donned the crusaders' cross and sword and went off to the Holy Land in defence of their 'Lady'. Their 'Lady' was often seen as a secret love, repeating the theme of the necessity for secrecy of the Magdalene's existence. French philosopher and critic gives credence to this theory as he states that the troubadours were essentially Cathars and later subject to the Inquisition. It isn't a huge stretch of the imagination to see the Dompna of their songs as the 'Lady' to whom their churches were dedicated.

For the most part simple farmers, the Cathars learned of the alternative teachings of Christ from travelling clerics called Cathari, who lived simply and humbly in the way taught by Jesus himself. They believed that these teachings were untainted by 'modern' thought and were purer and nearer to the truth dispensed on the shores of Galilee. They believed that spiritual transformation or advancement began in the mind and heart and how a person lived his life. They honoured Jesus as Messiah and anointed Son of God but as fully human, and baptism and church attendance was not enough to secure them a place in the Kingdom of Heaven.

Their religion was practiced in their everyday lives and not confined to extravagant display in a church. So entrenched in their beliefs were they, the Vatican did not rest until a war had been waged against the Cathars which ended in a massacre at Montsegur, again in the heart of France, where over two hundred Cathars were burned at the stake because they would not renounce their beliefs, including their belief in a Christ married to Mary Magdalene. It is from this background of fanaticism of the Catholic Church that we see the Inquisition born in 1233, when thousands of 'heretics' were tortured and killed in the effort to destroy all beliefs that were contrary to Mother Church (a term I find incongruous in light of the attitudes, surely Father Church would be more appropriate).

The Languedoc region of France was a nexus of Grail legend and associated Magdalene worship centred around Rennes-Le-Chateau. In 1209 an army of 30,000 soldiers under the auspices of Rome arrived in the region to slaughter the Cathari, decreed by Pope Innocent II as heretics. The Cathars were essentially Gnostics in their beliefs and the war against them raged on for thirty five years, resulting in the slaughter of many thousands and ending with the massacre at Montsegur where over two hundred Cathars were burned at the stake for heresy. Outwardly the Cathars were eradicated by the holy edict of Rome charged with blasphemy but the truth was opposite to the charges. In today's terms they were non-conformist needing no authority from the Catholic Church taking their teachings directly from the words of Christ. Their beliefs and practices were in fact endorsed by St Bernard who said, *'No sermons are more Christian than theirs and their morals are pure.'* The Catholic Church it seemed was prepared to annihilate what it couldn't suppress. The murder extended to any who showed support for the Cathars which effectively took care of most of the Languedoc population.

The Magdalene, it seems, was also revered in the heavens, as medieval astronomers assigned to her the planet Venus, the planet associated with Love and the Goddess. Venus traces a perfect five pointed star in the heavens as it travels through the night sky and it is a perfect pentacle that can be seen in the sacred geometry of Rennes-Le-Chateau's position amongst the mountains of France. (Key to the Sacred Pattern by Henry Lincoln).

Here lies the connection to the unfolding of our destiny right here and right now. The Christ Consciousness is emerging at a time when many are convinced that we are living at the dawn of the 'end times', as prophecies of the approach of the apocalypse are fulfilled daily on our TV screens as tsunamis, massive earthquakes and hurricanes, wars and famine. The New Age is certainly upon us and one symbol of that New Age – is Venus.

In the year 2012 an alignment will take place in the heavens between Earth and Venus following a transit that began in 2004. This alongside the fact that the Mayan calendar predicts the end of time on December 21st, the Winter Solstice, in 2012, a calendar which had its inception with the birth of Venus, forges a link once again with the return of the Goddess at a time when Venus is at its closest to Earth for many centuries. The return of the feminine principle in the divine, bringing unity and balance once again to the masculine/feminine energies, is echoed in the union of God/Goddess, Christ/Magdalene story. Indeed, a sacred re-union. With the Venus transit beginning in 2004 it seems appropriate that Dan Brown's *Da Vinci Code* emerged at that time too, heralding major new interest in the Magdalene.

In these uncertain times, where biblical prophesies of the end times are becoming apparent, something else is happening too. There is much talk of ascension and how it can be achieved, we are told that our very DNA is changing. So what does that all mean? And what does it have to do with Mary Magdalene?

Ascension is the process whereby our souls evolve to the next stage of being, out of the physical and into a 'light' body, in other words we are evolving to live as energy rather than matter. If what we are told is correct, we are not all ready for this change right now and the process is subtle unless conscious effort is made towards the evolution. There can be no doubt that our world is being pushed ever near to the precipice of extinction as wars ravage the planet and humanity, famines go unchecked when the storehouses of the world overflow, compassion is something that seems to be in the minority instead of in every heart. Our politicians duel daily over wealth, land and oil stocks, when these things will mean nothing in the great scheme of things. The Christ message is clear, love is the answer, Universal Love and love of each other at grass roots level. Marriage has become a thing of the past in favour of casual relationships that have no basis in human love, when in fact sacred sex in a loving stable relationship can open the door to the ascension process and the evolution of the soul.

So, where in all this, does the Magdalene fit in? She was the wife/lover of Christ, his first apostle appointed to spread the true teachings of Christ until she was silenced for two millennia by Peter and his Roman Church. Now, as human consciousness awakes to the sound of Goddess music and planetary alignments bring Venus close to Earth, we are beginning to feel the higher frequency energies associated with her teachings.

It is her time.

Whilst this is part of the Magdalene mystery it isn't the main subject of this book, but there are countless websites and published books that give more information than can be covered within these pages.

We find an oblique reference to this sacred re-union and return of the sacred feminine in the pages of the scriptures, in Isaiah 62:1-4

'For Zion's sake I will not be silent, for Jerusalem's sake I will not remain quiet, until her righteousness shines out like the dawn, her salvation like a blazing torch. The nations will see

your righteousness, and all kings your glory; you will be called
by a new name that the mouth of the Lord will give to you. You
will be a crown of splendour in the Lord's hand, a royal
diadem in the hand of your God.'

I have no doubt that the new name that will be given to her is
'Magdalene'.

Chapter Five

The Gospel of Mary Magdalene

Brief and fragmented it may be, but the Gospel of Mary Magdalene in its survived state is nothing less than a clarion call to humanity to awaken to the teachings and words of Jesus Christ in a way that is simply that; a way of being, that the Christ message drew from the source of creation, 'I am the way, the truth and the life'. Now at the dawn of an age where enlightenment has bred nothing more than discontent, terror, violence, and disrespect for our planet earth and humanity itself, it is a beacon that can change the fears and hopes of millions as it has done for the past two millennia. How many of us have become acclimatised to shut out any spiritual meaning or message in our lives? How many of us can still hear the truth and majesty in Christ's message of love? The Gospel of Mary is just one of the now famous Gnostic gospels and its discovery and availability now can point us in the direction of understanding the teachings that changed the world.

In every spiritual tradition or religion there are teachings that are a trumpet blast for all to hear, should we choose to, and the raw power of the message of Christ is no different and who better to continue with the tradition and the teachings but the one whom he entrusted the task to, on the morning of his resurrection?

We have become all too deaf to the spiritual call from within ourselves but Jesus is actually teaching us to recognise and acknowledge that divinity within us in every breath of his teaching. The Gospel brings to life the inner workings and relationships of the mind, the soul and the spirit.

Peter has come to us down the ages as the intermediary, the preacher, repeating and spreading the words of Jesus, Mary now shows us that we are in fact in contact with the Divine and need no intermediary. Peter and the other apostles work on the outer connections on a mental level, Mary shows us the inner pathway and transformation and development of the soul.

Along with the other gospels found at Nag Hammadi, the Gospels of Phillip, Thomas, Bartholomew, the Gospel of Mary Magdalene was rejected by the Roman Catholic Church then and now and branded as heresy. Dangerous to the power structures Christ detested? Yes, certainly. It is interesting though, that John, the disciple Christ entrusted with the care of his adored mother, quite obviously sees the Magdalene as the founder of Christianity at a time long before the dramatic conversion of Paul at Damascus. John, Chapter 20 makes this abundantly clear.

The first six pages of the manuscript of the Gospel of Mary Magdalene are missing and we are taken straight into the text where Mary is posing deep spiritual questions to Jesus. She asks him about matter "What is matter? Will it last forever?" Mary is asking a fundamental question about the existence of the world and its nature. Jesus replies to her *'All that is born, all that is created, all the elements of nature are interwoven and united with each other. All that is composed will be decomposed; everything returns to its origin. Those who have ears let them hear.'* This is the transmission of knowledge and understanding of human beings at one with the Father, the Source, the Divine. Jesus lived his entire life in intimate contact and relationship with God and by these teachings we too can regain that intimacy. He reminds us of the interdependence and impermanence of all matter. Everything, everybody, every life, is interconnected in a rich tapestry. When one strand of the tapestry is affected, so by connection, is the whole. *'All that is composed will be decomposed....'* reminds us that even the Universe is not permanent and will not last forever. It had a beginning and it will have an end.

Not having an understanding of the impermanence of matter, of all things created, projects us into the materialistic world full of false attachments and illusion that we live in today. It is that attachment to illusory things, the importance to us of the material that produces suffering in the world. It is questions of this depth that we find Mary asking right at the beginning of the surviving text.

Page seven finds Peter asking Jesus about the nature of sin, 'What is the sin of the world?' Christ's answer was clearly not what Peter wanted to hear, he tells him that there is no sin, it is us that make sin exist. In other words Nothing is sinful in its own essences, its how we use things in wrongful ways that create sin. Jean-Yves LeLoup explains in his commentary ' *We are responsible for the world in which we live, for in a deep sense it is we who create it, by interpreting it positively or negatively'.*

There is a common thread running through this page of the Gospel of Mary with that of St Paul's letter to the Romans.

Chapter seven voices an echo of the teaching that Christ delivered to Peter, who it seems missed the point entirely. As the text continues, Jesus is urging that no laws are imposed as that in itself would create sin as men would find that they could not abide by them. Hm, that's another one that missed the mark. In Mary's gospel, Jesus said, *'Do not add more laws to those given in the Torah lest you are bound by them.'* Paul states in Romans 7 *'But now we are delivered from the Laws, for we became dead to that which bound us.'* Mary's gospel has Jesus saying, *'There is no sin, It is you who makes sin exist.'* Paul says, *'For without Laws, sin is dead.'*

There follows deep and meaningful teachings from Jesus, and whilst vital to regaining the intimacy with the Source they are not the subject of this work and so we pass them to arrive on what is listed as page nine of the surviving text. *'The disciples were in great sorrow, shedding many tears, and saying: "How are we to go among the unbelievers and announce the gospel of the Kingdom of the Son of Man? They did not spare his life. Why should they spare ours?"'*

The disciples once again are entrenched in the fear for their own lives, and it is Mary, with her deeper understanding and experience of Christ that tries to comfort them and encourage them. Page nine continues, *'Then Mary arose, embraced them all, and began to speak to her brothers. "Do not remain in sorrow and doubt, for his grace will guide you and comfort you."'*

Mary's ease in comforting them comes from her understanding of the grace of Yeshua, its presence among them and its ability to protect them. She reminds them that reliance upon their own strength and personal ability will get them nowhere, but if they remain at one with the Source they will come to see and understand that something greater than all of them is at work in their lives. The text continues. *"Instead let us praise his greatness, for he has prepared us for this. He is calling us to be fully human."* Mary is explaining to the disciples the need to focus themselves in God/the Source/the Divine, instead of becoming wrapped up in their own physicality. She asks them to understand the bigger picture. She also reminds them that Christ's mission was centred on these teachings as he 'prepared them for this'.

'To become fully human' is important here. It reminds us of the purpose of the incarnation of Jesus; for the Divine to experience humanity in all its glory, in all its joys and all its sorrows, to embrace and balance within ourselves the masculine and feminine, to become whole. It is this wholeness that enables us to love from a state of abundance and not lack, the unconditional love that Jesus had for us all. It is in this state of peace that Mary displays her true and intimate knowledge and understanding of Jesus' teachings. Only with true understanding comes true peace.

Page ten of the Gospel shows Peter, having been comforted by Mary, asking her to share more of the higher teachings that she has received. He openly acknowledges that Mary had a special and intimate relationship with Jesus and that she was loved above all others. He shows her a respect that unfortunately doesn't last long, as true to character, once Mary begins to share her knowledge with them he reverts to his previous bullishness and refuses to listen to the higher truths.

It isn't difficult to see Mary as a contemplative person, grounded in her own humanity, at peace with her own shadow side, freed by Jesus when he 'cast out seven demons' from her. She was able to focus in silence on the teachings of Yeshua, find compassion there and become the female archetype of spiritual intercession. Along with her deep and intimate knowledge of death and dying, the transformational journey of the soul at the physical death, this has made Mary a worthy advocate of the sick and dying. She knows that Jesus will die, she follows him to his death on the cross and she is the first to witness the resurrection as she meets Jesus in his risen form. She reveals the mysteries, and is worthy of becoming the Sophia to the Logos of Jesus.

The following pages are in explanation of the nature and relationship of the body, the soul and the spirit and how it is the higher mind, the spirit, that perceives and experiences the Spirit of God (Pneuma). Mary passes on her knowledge of the development and progress of the soul through what she calls many climates. The disciples will have none of it, maintaining it to be her imagination and nothing else, still unable to accept the fact that Jesus had taught Mary about things which they could not even begin to imagine, once again proving her superior understanding and intellect. They had shared much with Jesus, hardships, hunger, thirst, vilification, food, bread and wine, so how could it be that he had not shared these things if they were fact. True to form, it is Peter who challenges Mary. It is Andrew though who accuses her of false teachings, saying he did not believe that Jesus would speak like that at all.

Jesus had preferred to teach the disciples in parables related to their own experience because these men were honest and humble fishermen of Galilee, and although they perhaps did not understand the teachings immediately, they would come to see their meanings later. The teachings that Yeshua shared with Mary however, would not have been understood by them on any level and so he did not face them with the confusion that would have ensued.

Page eighteen shows us Mary's grief at Peter's non belief in her. *Then Mary wept, and answered him, "My brother Peter, what can you be thinking? Do you believe that this is my imagination, that I invented this vision? Or do you believe that I would lie about our Teacher?"*

Mary is crying out of frustration, like a small child who has shared something wonderful and awesome with one she loves only to be scorned or told that it is all in her imagination. We see Mary calling Peter her brother, another indication that there is no hierarchy among the disciples and certainly no indication that Peter is the automatic leader of the group, let alone a superior figure such as a bishop or pope. He is simply a brother who has caused pain to Mary through his own disbelief and hurtful words.

Can we not see reflected in this bickering and closed mindedness, the picture of division and contention between churches and denominations today, all within the Christian faith, let alone those of other faiths?

Perhaps it is the understanding of Mary that will lead us into the Kingdom as she continues to share the teachings of her beloved Yeshua, unadulterated, untainted and pure.

There are several transcripts and translations of the Gospel of Mary Magdalene but I have found the version translated from the Coptic by Jean-Yves LeLoup by far the most lucid and easily understood format.

Chapter Six

Beyond Nag Hammadi

Found in Nag Hammadi in 1945, the gnostic gospels, or what
have now become known as the Nag Hammadi Library,
consisted of thirteen different codices, within which were fifty
sacred texts. These texts were hidden to preserve them at a
time when the search for orthodoxy within the early church
would brook no mention of the higher teachings of Christ and
sought to eradicate all trace of them. Texts such as the Gospel
of Thomas, the Gospel of Phillip, the Gospel of the Truth, the
Dialogue of the Saviour, all contain truths that are now
considered heresies. These early sacred texts were not
intended to survive, the emerging orthodox church needed
conformity and patriarchal line of succession so the gnostic
teachers and their documents were persecuted and destroyed.
Well, almost.

Pistis Sophia was not among the documents discovered at Nag Hammadi, it was in fact published far earlier, in 1921 making it the first gnostic text to exist in English. Unlike the Nag Hammadi library which consists mainly of 'Gospels', *Pistis Sophia* is a story about the fall of humanity from beings of a spiritual nature to the world of matter. In effect it expounds the theory that we are essentially spirit that has become entrapped in matter and how we are trying to awaken to our plight and free ourselves and return home. There is a striking similarity in the content of Pistis Sophia and many of the web sites and books that are bringing us information on the evolution of the soul into light body and being able to free ourselves from the physical. It seems purely a matter of perspective. *Pistis Sophia* is an attempt to awaken us to our true nature, to awaken our sleeping souls however difficult that may be whilst we are hampered by the density of our physical bodies and out of synch with the higher frequencies of the world of spirit.

Sophia means 'Wisdom', she is the Divine Feminine set to return and is identified with Mary Magdalene. This 'gospel' resonates with us at this time, striking a chord of recognition deep within, regardless of religious or spiritual background. In the *Book of Wisdom of Solomon* from the Apocrypha, Sophia or Wisdom is seen as a female figure, one who was created before time, who co-creates the world with God and shares his throne. She intercedes with God on our behalf and attempts to return those who do not know God to him. In this way, she is also recognised by the Church of the Latter Day Saints and Heavenly Mother.

It is within the pages of *Pistis Sophia* that we find yet another source of the Magdalene/Yeshua story. It also contains confirmation of the antagonism of Peter to Mary and also from other male disciples. It is clear from this text that Peter loathed the Magdalene. His antipathy to women generally leaps from the test, especially in Chapter Six when he states

'*My Lord, let the women cease to question in order that we may also question*'. *More specifically, towards Mary's prominence, Peter's anger is blatant. He says, 'My Lord, we will not endure this woman, for she taketh the opportunity from us .... '.* Later, Mary apologises to Jesus and asks that he '*be not wrath with me if I question on all things.*' Jesus' reply is that she should '*Question what thou wilt.*'

Further evidence of the chasm between Mary and Peter and in a more sinister vein the physical threat that was only hinted at in the Gospel of Mary. The Magdalene is talking with Jesus about her understanding of his teachings when she then says, '*but I am afraid of Peter, because he threatened me and hateth our sex.*' The open hostility from Peter seems to have weighed heavily on the author that it bears the ring of truth in it. The antagonism seems only to have been contained by Jesus himself, and so after his death, Peter was free to begin the hatchet job on Mary and the other female disciples. Peter's problem with women is not mere speculation. The bible itself tells us that he was so afraid of his own daughter's sexuality that he prayed hard until such a time as she became paralysed and then was unable to lie with any man.

The tension between the two and the revelation that he had threatened her gives us insight into how much on the edge she must have lived her life after Christ's death. Without the protection of Jesus, she was clearly in danger. Putting together all of the messages contained in the Bible and the gnostic texts, we have a picture of Peter as less than super intelligent and a nasty tempered bully to boot.

Even Jesus loses his patience with Peter's inability to 'get it'. In Mark's gospel we find Jesus at the end of his tether with Peter as he challenges the Lord when he predicts his rejection by the chief priests and elders and his subsequent death. 31And he began to teach them, that the Son of man must suffer many things, and be rejected of the elders, and of the chief priests, and scribes, and be killed, and after three days rise again.[32] And he spoke that saying openly. And Peter took him, and began to rebuke him.[33] But when he had turned about and looked on his disciples, he rebuked Peter, saying, *'Get thee behind me, Satan: for thou savourest not the things that be of God, but the things that be of men.'*

We saw, in the Gospel of Mary Magdalene, how peter sought to undermine Mary as she recounted her vision of Jesus and his subsequent teaching, when Peter implies that she has made it all up.

Pistis Sophia is not easy to read and even less easy to understand, but there are several outstanding passages that convey the essence of the work, mostly when the main characters come to life with a voice.

In it, Jesus states quite clearly, *'Mary, thou blessed one, whom I will perfect in all mysteries of those of the height, discourse in openness, thou, whose heart is raised to the Kingdom of Heaven more than all my brethren.'* He later says, *Where I shall be, there will also be my twelve ministers. But Mary Magdalene and John, the virgin, will tower over all men who shall receive my mysteries. And they will be on my right and on my left. And I am they, and they are I.'*

I'd say that was a pretty clear indication of the ranking of the Magdalene in Jesus' eyes, wouldn't you? It also gives added credence to the fact that there were two distinct churches within early Christianity. The Petrine or open, orthodox church and the Johannine Church which was said to have been formed by John and the Magdalene, teaching the secrets of the soul to those who had the intelligence, the imagination, and the 'ears to hear'.

Evidence would seem to point to the fact that Jesus was not averse to proclaiming the superiority of Mary to all around him, and it doesn't take a strong imagination to understand the feelings of the rough and ready fishermen of Galilee. Unfortunately, Mary appears not to have suffered fools gladly and did appear to monopolise Jesus whenever they were gathered together to receive teaching, and this couldn't have helped the situation much.

The translation of these texts was completed in 1970 and now we have an insight into the life and work of the first Christians.

The Magdalene appears prominently in several of the Nag Hammadi discoveries, such as the Gospel of Phillip, the Gospel of Thomas, and The Dialogue of the Saviour.

From the Gospel of Phillip we see the true relationship of Jesus and the Magdalene emerge. *'As for the Wisdom who is called "the barren," she is the mother of the angels. And the companion of the Saviour was Mary Magdalene. The Lord loved her more than all the disciples, and used to kiss her often on her mouth. The rest of the disciples [...]. They said to him "Why do you love her more than all of us?" The Saviour answered and said to them, "Why do I not love you like her? When a blind man and one who sees are both together in darkness, they are no different from one another. When the light comes, then he who sees will see the light, and he who is blind will remain in darkness.'*

Not only the intimate relationship but the intellectual relationship emerges too. Mary is obviously far more in tune with the higher teachings of Christ.

Chapter Seven

Peter Vs. Mary

To examine this question in the fullest light, we must revisit some of the points made in earlier chapters, for which I apologise, but for the sake of coherence I believe their mention to be of relevance.

It is apparent at the shortest of glances that politics had reared its ugly head even in the early church, as some of the early Christians revered the Magdalene as the Apostle to the Apostles and other factions simply chose to give her no apostolic recognition whatsoever instead preferring to brand her a reformed prostitute, for which we have seen there is no biblical basis.

In her ground-breaking book *Mary Magdalene, First Apostle* Anne Graham Brock quotes Hippolytus, one of the early Christian bishops, as saying, '*Lest the female apostles doubt the angels, Christ himself came to them so that the women would be apostles of Christ and by their obedience rectify the ancient sin of Eve ....Christ showed himself to the male apostles and said, 'It is I who appeared to these women and I who wanted to send them to you as apostles.'* It seems pretty self explanatory to me. There were accepted female apostles within the early church.

So how did the early church define an apostle? Clearly, from all early writings, an apostle was determined by a resurrection appearance of Christ, as claimed by Paul on his journey to Damascus. If that is so, then the Magdalene, as being the very first to witness the resurrection, be acclaimed as first apostle. As we have seen previously though, there is dissent amongst the canonical gospels as to this fact.

Hebraic tradition uses the term as an indicator of being an official messenger – again, the Magdalene was sent to give the good news to the rest of the disciples. St Paul himself defends his own claim to apostleship with the requirement of two factors, as we have already seen, the witnessing of the resurrected Jesus and receipt of a divine call or commission to proclaim Christ's message. Certainly we see within Paul's writings, a clear link between those who have witnessed the risen Christ, and therefore legitimate apostles, and Jesus himself. This was an powerful link which give legitimacy to texts concerning any particular apostle This has only served to highlight rivalry between apostles for authority and research has shown that this related particularly to Peter and Mary Magdalene beginning what has become a controversial topic as we awaken to the call of the New Age whereby spiritual truth is becoming the new Grail.

A translation from the Greek writings of Gregory of Antioch shows Jesus as appearing to the Magdalene and to Mary, Jesus' mother, at the tomb and proclaiming, *'Be the first teachers to the teachers. So that Peter who denied me learns that I can also choose women apostles.'* Whatever the source of Gregory's information, one thing is clear, that women's entitlement to be apostles was being defended right back as far as 593 AD when Gregory put his quill to parchment. Not only that, his work highlights the controversy begun with Peter's absolute refusal to recognise women apostles as such.

As we already know, the canonical gospels vary as to those that acknowledge the Magdalene as the first witness and the one which designates Peter as first witness. It was not until the discovery at Nag Hammadi of the works now recognised as Gnostic Gospels that we find further corroboration of the Magdalene as the first true witness and therefore apostle. Human nature being as it is, even back at the time of the early church, will come down in favour of one or the other and this in turn must colour any documents or testimonies that are issued in the light of one or other way of perception.

The majority of the Gospel of Luke gives pride of place to Peter by the use of three distinct methods. Firstly, by adding material found nowhere else, that gives credence to Peter, secondly by omitting anything unfavourable to Peter, found in many other verses of scripture and by adjusting the story to fit the ethos of the author of Luke's gospel.

To justify that statement, we only need to look at how Peter's role is enhanced during his first encounter with Jesus. In Luke's version, Jesus says, '*I will make you catch men*', using the singular of 'you', as though addressing himself to Peter only. Yet, the other gospels all agree with the use of the plural of 'you', when they relate the same incident as Jesus saying, '*I will make you fishers* (plural) *of men*'. The adjustment occurs most blatantly as in the three other canonical gospels, Jesus predicts Peter's denial of him, it is only in Luke's gospel that Jesus gives a reason in mitigation of this. '*But I have prayed for you in order that your faith may not fail*'.

In contrast, we see Mary Magdalene losing her true status, in Luke only, as the first witness, in favour of Peter. The author seeks to diminish her status in very subtle ways. The other synoptic gospels refer to the Magdalene at the crucifixion as amongst the women that had ministered to him (Jesus), whereas Luke asserts that she ministered to 'them' (the disciples). Whilst this may appear to be nit-picking its subtlety continues in his description of her as someone who was healed by Jesus and now provided financial support. Whilst this latter part is true, the Magdalene had family wealth which she put at Jesus' disposal; it places her firmly where the early church doctrine accepts women, as bene-factors and carers, not as leaders.

Similarly, the other three gospels name Mary Magdalene as being at the foot of the cross; Luke merely designates them as *'women who followed Jesus from Galilee'*. It is Luke's gospel alone that refers to *'all his acquaintances'* as standing witness to the horrors of the crucifixion, whereas the other three agree completely that the male disciples fled leaving the women alone to bear witness to his suffering, including by name, Mary Magdalene.

The last obvious snub by Luke is at the commissioning of Mary, agreed by all three other gospels, as he completely omits it from existence. This not only denies Mary the status of witness to the resurrection but also the role of messenger commissioned by Jesus to take the teachings and news to the others. In this manner Luke sets the seal on women's role within the church, giving a tenuous hook on which to hang the argument for male only apostles.

Even though Luke's gospel does give more space to women than the others it is in the detrimental role as followers not leaders, in contrast to John's gospel which portrays strong female leadership and never once gives an exclusive male list of disciples. It is in this gospel we find the Samaritan woman at the well charged by Jesus to take his teachings to Samaria. The crucial sequence of events at the tomb is given to us by the author of John's gospel in a way that brooks no misunderstanding. John 20:1 states *'early on the first day of the week, whilst it was still dark, Mary Magdalene went to the tomb and saw that the stone had been removed from the entrance'*.

All the above could just come down to a person's preference, Luke or John. But there is so much other documentation in the canonical gospels, the Gnostic gospels and other contemporary writing that gives credence to the Johannine version. In Matthew's gospels, Jesus rebukes Peter, calls him Satan, and refers to him as a stumbling block, though the author does hedge his bets rather as he gives credence to the Magdalene as first witness but portrays Peter as primary leader despite the admonitions and obvious loss of patience with him by Jesus. Interestingly, Matthew makes no mention of Peter after his denial of Christ; he isn't even mentioned when Jesus sends his disciples out into the world.

Not surprisingly the only other text to reflect the work of Luke's author is the apocryphal Gospel of Peter.

The gnostic Gospel of Thomas gives rise to yet another debate. It is within this text we find Peter saying to Jesus, *'Let Mary leave us, because women are not worthy of life'*. I doubt he meant that women were not worthy to live but rather referred to a 'spiritual life'. In either case, Jesus defends Mary when he says, *'Look, I myself shall lead her so that I will make her male in order that she too may become a living spirit resembling you males.'* These words have centred themselves in scholarly debate as to their meaning. Clearly Jesus did not intent to make Mary physically male. It is far more likely that he was telling Peter that gender had no bearing on spiritual worthiness or authority. Whatever the reason, Jesus fairly and squarely refutes Peter in defence of Mary.

In the Gospel of Mary there is an insight into her spirituality as she continues to receive visions and teachings from Christ who praises her for 'not wavering', as she is revealed as an authority figure and continuer of the traditions as she shares her knowledge with the others and comforts them. She is successful in her mission as she *turns them towards the good, and they begin to discuss the words of the saviour*. Whilst it is Peter who asks Mary to share her knowledge it is also he that attacks her about the truth of her statements. She is defended by Levi, who accuses Peter of acting like an adversary and being his usual hot tempered self.

In *Pistis Sophia*, Peter is still whinging on about women in general and Mary in particular. 'My Lord, we are not able to suffer this woman who takes the opportunity from us and speaks many times' and 'My Lord, let the women cease to question, that we may also question.' His bitterness and jealousy are reflected in the passages of the Gospel of Mary when he asks if the Saviour would really reveal secret teachings to a woman and not to the men. 'Are we to turn and listen to her? Did he prefer her to us?' Peter is desperately trying to defend his position to the other disciples as Mary comes into the ascendance. Poor Peter, I think he would have a really bad time of it today!

In the passages of The Dialogue of the saviour Mary is highly praised, and Jesus refers to her as being worthy, and like her teacher.

The ascendance of Mary is most clearly seen in *Pistis Sophia* where she holds a prominent role amongst the disciples as the one who is foremost in discussions with the Master. After Peter's complaints about Mary, there is an occasion where Mary seeks to defend her position, as she relates Peter's intimidation of her. She tells Jesus that she understood that she was able to question and understand his teachings although she was physically afraid of Peter, *'My Lord, my mind is understanding at all times that I should come forward at any time and give the interpretation of the words which Sophia spoke, but I am afraid of Peter, for he threatens me, and hates my gender.'*

The words employed in this passage are emotive and colourful, such as 'hate' and 'threaten' and give a clearer picture of Peter's disposition.

The Gospels of Phillip and the Gospel of Mary reflect further Mary's true status within the group. As the Gospel of Mary tells us, Peter said to Mary, *'Sister, we know that you have been loved extensively by the saviour as no other woman'*, and later, Levi's defence of Mary against Peter further illustrates this point, as he states that Jesus loved her more than all the disciples, not more than other women, but all the disciples.

Once again, in *Pistis Sophia*, Mary is elevated as primary figure, *'Mariam, the Blessed one, whom I will complete in all the mysteries of the height, speak openly, you are she whose heart is more directed to the kingdom of heaven, than all your brothers'*. Scholars agree that 'Mariam, the blessed one, is Mary Magdalene and not the mother of Jesus as the passage continues, *'After these things Mary, the Mother of Jesus, also came forward.'*

The 4th century document in Greek, The Acts of Phillip further shed light on the prominence of Mary as we find her 'present at the side of Christ when he allocates the missions to the apostles.' We are told that she holds the register of all the countries and it is Mary that prepares the bread and salt and breaks the bread. Is this an illustration of her administering the Eucharist? Within this text, Christ sends Mary with Phillip to 'encourage him with love and compassion'.

More dramatically, and controversially, late in this work, Mary is found fighting a dragon as she performs a ritual of exorcism Along with Bartholomew she holds a chalice and sprinkles the demon whilst making the sign of the cross.

The Acts of Phillip show a healing, whereby Phillip puts his finger in Mary's mouth and then proceeds to heal Stachys, thereby indicating that Mary's saliva has healing properties. Following this incident, Phillip is described as baptising the men present, and Mary, the women.

Examination of these early writings in conjunction with the canonical gospels gives a clear picture of Mary as a primary figure of authority and priesthood in the early church, due to several factors; her true relationship to Jesus, his admiration and commissioning of her, her crystal clear understanding of the teachings of the Saviour, and evidence of later church authorities deliberate erasure or diminishing of Mary within canon and tradition.

The Apostolic Succession from Peter favoured by the Roman Catholic Church is patriarchal and flawed, but perhaps the time is now that the Magdalene will return to the consciousness of man as the representative of the Sacred Feminine part of the Divine. Long may she reign.

Chapter Eight

Who Was the Beloved Disciple?

An unexpected avenue of thought cropped up during my research for this book. I came across several scholars (in particular Raymond E Brown) who believed, and put up a convincing argument, that the Magdalene was in fact the author of the fourth gospels, the Gospel of John, the evidence for which is considerable. In fact, there is more evidence for Mary being the author than there is for John. Most theologians and biblical scholars agree that the fourth gospel shows clear signs of editing, shuffling, additions and insertions and it is widely accepted that this gospel was a result of lengthy development rather than a straightforward writing down of events.

This aspect of the Magdalene story also lays to rest another ghost that has haunted the halls of Christian myth. The

Beloved Apostle is a title that has been bestowed on John, giving rise to some extreme anti-Christians concluding quite without foundation, that Jesus had a homosexual relationship with John! Quite apart from the fact that there is absolutely no evidence, other than the 'Beloved' title, there is so much evidence to the contrary and that our Magdalene was his lover and wife.

We have seen, via the canonical Gospels and the Gnostic Gospel, along with other contemporary writings that women, in particular Mary Magdalene, played a prominent role in the early church and that their contribution has been suppressed to suit the patriarchal foundation of the same. The Magdalene has suffered the most in this way, because she contributed the most. Is her authorship of the fourth gospel under the name of John, her way of making her voice heard, and by association, was she the founder of the Johannine Community?

Let's see if the evidence stacks up?

Firstly, we need to acknowledge that the canonical gospels were not necessarily authored by those that gave their name to those scriptures. Theologians agree that the gospels were written from first hand knowledge of the disciple whose name the gospel in written in, or from oral tradition and handed down knowledge from a person or persons who knew that disciple, written to express the ideas and information of the one in whose name it is written.

The leading Catholic Scripture scholar, Raymond E Brown believes that the fourth gospel was penned by an anonymous follower of Jesus who was widely known as the Beloved Disciple, or simply, the Beloved. Whoever the Beloved was, they knew Jesus intimately and became the founder of the Johannine Community, whose history is strongly linked to the issue of ownership of the fourth gospel.

It is clear from reading the Gospel of John that it differs in style and content from the other three canonical gospels. It is firstly an account of Jesus' ministry and secondly a story of the community. Following Jesus' execution, resurrection and ascension the Jewish Christians were expelled from the synagogues, thereby separating them from the Jewish communities and putting them in a dangerous situation. Every person who was not Jewish in those times was expected to worship Caesar. Being seen as outside the Jewish system, they were therefore in this category and as they had no intention of worshipping Caesar, they were at risk from the military and political machines. The reason for their expulsion from the synagogues was their insistence on the divinity of Jesus. Its founder was the disciple known as the Beloved Disciple, or The disciple Jesus Loved.

It is this focus on the true identity and divinity of Christ that is central to the fourth gospel. The other gospels recount the miracles performed by Jesus and restrict his dialogue to short sentences or parables, whereas in John we find Jesus talking at great length with the disciples and the author has written in much more detail about the miracles, seeing them as signs of the divinity of Jesus and looks deeper into their true significance.

The Beloved Disciple appears in significant passages of the fourth gospel, firstly, in 13:23-26 where we find reference to 'the disciple whom Jesus loved'. As Jesus ministry and teachings were all about loving each other unconditionally, there is clearly something special about this disciple to warrant singling out in this manner. Indeed Jesus loved all of his disciples. This is a reference perhaps to a different kind of love, an intimate love as would be seen between husband and wife. This disciple is sitting next to Jesus at the Last Supper, and it is for this reason that we find controversy in the identity of this disciple being identified as the Magdalene in Leonardo Da Vinci's masterpiece. This character has been deliberately portrayed with overt feminine characteristics despite protestations to the contrary. As I said previously, there is no way that the Magdalene would not have been present on this occasion. It is this 'disciple who Jesus loved', that asks Christ to reveal who it is that will betray him.

In John 18:15-16, although there is no specific reference to the Beloved Disciple, the character concerned in this passage is clearly known as one having a special relationship with Jesus. The scene is following the arrest of Jesus, and it is this disciple that is seen talking to the gatekeeper and securing entry to the High Priest's courtyard. Peter is at first denied access.

Why then, in certain passages is the Beloved Disciple clearly male? Many scholars believe that this is a result of careful editing by the community after the event. Remember that the emerging church was formed in days of patriarchal extremism and to have a female founder would have been difficult for the members of the community. Jesus after all taught unconditional love and equality for all, including women and approved of women taking positions of leadership. This attitude was probably the most controversial and unpalatable to mainstream thought.

On reading the fourth gospel, it is clear that for whatever reason the identity of the Beloved Disciple, the Disciple Jesus Loved, had to be kept a secret. Why? Because early church fathers including the remaining members of the community needed to erase any reference to the Magdalene and Christ having been married.

The ethos of the fourth gospel has much more in common with the Nag Hammadi Library than it does with the synoptic gospels. The Gnostic Gospels, as we have seen, are physical evidence of early writings which endorse the Jesus/Magdalene theory and the Magdalene is also given prominence in John's

Gospel. The Johannine Community endorsed the belief that a person could commune directly with God and needed no intermediary, and all spiritual experience and revelation was very much an individual experience. They were entrenched in the mechanics of the soul and the high Christology of Jesus. All of these are reflected dramatically in the Gospel of Mary Magdalene.

We know that the Magdalene had to, for her own safety, flee the country and therefore would have handed the community over. In fact the community appears to have undergone three distinct phases of construct and leadership. The first phase of the original group was under the leadership of Mary, until such time as she had to leave, being honoured and respected as the First Apostle and as the partner or wife of Jesus.

The second stage of the community appears to have an oral tradition of their gospel, including the fact that the Magdalene was their founder and leader. It is likely that by this time Mary has died in France. It is around this time also, that a split appears to develop within the community, based on the difference of opinion as to the divinity of Jesus. There is now two distinct 'camps' within the Johannine community.

These two groups became known as the Apostolic Christians and the Secessionists. The Apostolic Christians sought acceptance by the early Orthodox Church. They claim that their original leader was a female disciple of Jesus but that she was superseded by male leadership due this desire for acceptance. They appear to have been the sect that gave rise to the belief that their gospel was rewritten to hide the truth about the Magdalene.

The Secessionists were the bigger of the two groups who held firm to the Magdalene tradition and to the fact that she was not only the Beloved Disciple but also the author of the fourth gospel. They were allied to other Gnostic groups and their doctrine is reflected in much of the Gnostic Gospels as found at Nag Hammadi. They also identify Mary as the Disciple that Jesus loved.

Much of the evidence to Mary being the author of the fourth gospel is found in the Nag Hammadi writings especially within the pages of the Gospel of Phillip and the Gospel of Mary. Over and over gain these texts refer to the Magdalene as being the disciple who Jesus loved the most which is in direct contradiction to the belief that John was 'the disciple Jesus loved'

There are three possibilities which explain the direct contradictions between the other three canonical gospels and the fourth gospel, One is that there were two traditions developing, as we have just seen, and that the differences simply reflect that. Or the Gnostic writings were written in direct response to the fourth gospel and these writers have assumed that because Mary is featured so prominently in this gospel that she is the Beloved Disciple. Raymond Brown prefers this explanation, believing that the Gnostics gave birth to this idea for that very reason. This theory is dependant upon the fourth gospel was written before the Nag Hammadi texts.

The other possibility, which ties in with everything else we know of the Magdalene so far, and that is that Mary's life would be under threat if it became known that she was the wife of Jesus and as is being explored, she had given birth and so continue the Christ bloodline. They would have wanted all reference to her true relationship removed from the public domain and yet still want their gospel to be accepted. It is also a fact that any 'gospel' written by a woman, would in those days, find little credence with the emerging church fathers.

There can be no proof at this time about the reasons for the contradictions or the mystery of the Beloved Disciple, but I come down in favour of the last alternative as it fits with everything else that has been discovered and is still being discovered about the Magdalene.

The question has to be asked, why not remove all reference to Mary Magdalene instead of doctoring the existing references? The fact that Mary was the first apostle, was also at the foot of the cross, had been the one to anoint Jesus as the Christ and had been, at the very least such an ardent follower, that to eradicate her entirely would have caused more problems of diversity from the other three gospels. Mary was present at the three most important events in the Jesus story, the Anointing, The Crucifixion and the Resurrection and is shown to be so by Matthew, Mark and Luke. However, it seems important to maintain knowledge that the community was founded by the 'Beloved Disciple', thereby accounting further for the alteration of the texts to portray this character as male. This would also account for Mary Magdalene appearing alongside the 'Beloved Disciple' in some of the passages. By making it appear that she is two different people, the person rewriting the text achieves the desired effect.

The fourth gospel gives a clearer timeline of Jesus' ministry and it is from this text that the traditional idea of his ministry being over three years. It is in the Gospel of John only that three different Feasts of the Passover are mentioned. The other gospels only mention the Passover that occurs at the beginning of the crucifixion. We also see Jesus moving about the country much more in the fourth gospel as he is told of travelling between Galilee to Jerusalem, to Samaria before returning to Galilee, then to Jerusalem, Galilee, across the Jordan, Bethany, Ephraim, back to Bethany and thence to Jerusalem where he was eventually arrested and crucified. The synoptic gospels show Jesus in ministry mainly in Galilee then to Jerusalem where after a very short time he is arrested.

At the end of the fourth gospel there is a strange reference to the 'Disciple Jesus Loved'. *'Peter turned and saw that the Disciple Jesus Loved was following them.* (This was the one who had leaned against Jesus at the Supper and had said to Jesus, 'Lord, who is going to betray you?') *When Peter saw him, he asked, 'Lord, what about him? Jesus answered him 'If I want him to remain alive until I come again what is that to you? You must follow me.'* (John 21:20-22)

The writer has gone to a great deal of trouble to identify the Disciple Jesus Loved without actually giving a name. The lengthy description of the disciple leaning against him at the Last Supper seems out of place and unnecessary here. Jesus' reply seems more a rebuke to Peter than an explanation. It is unlikely that his words are to be taken literally, that the disciple would never die. Rather it is another request of Jesus that this disciple be always remembered and revered for what she was, the Beloved of Jesus and the First Apostle, as he had requested after the Anointing, when he asked that 'wherever the gospel is preached she be remembered for this.'

There seem to be more reasons to attribute the authorship of the fourth gospel to Mary than to John and to designate her as the Beloved Disciple. It will remain a matter for conjecture until further texts come to light, which I have no doubt, they will.

Chapter Nine

Black Madonas

Throughout history, we see Mary Magdalene portrayed as having fair hair, anything from blonde through to red, fair of skin and voluptuous if not sexy in appearance. Yet there is a connection with what we see in parts of Europe and beyond, with the cults of the Black Madonna.

Mary, we are told was a woman of Jewish descent from the countryside of Palestine, surely blonde hair was not typical of this region, she would surely have been olive skinned, dark eyed and dark haired as were most of those from this area, in fact the classic Semitic appearance. Also, in our search for the real Magdalene we have learned that she most probably spent some time in Egypt, the sun-baked deserts enhancing her already dark olive appearance.

But on closer inspection, it goes deeper than that.

During my quest for the real Mary Magdalene, I was surprised by the numerous connections made to the Black Madonna cults that were widespread in Europe and although, I confess, I initially dismissed this line of research as irrelevant, although I have now come to realise the importance of the Madonnas and their shrines.

To find the missing piece of the puzzle we need to explore further back in history and religion to understand the symbolism of the Black Madonna, for symbolic, she surely is. It is interesting to note, that wonderful man of God, Pope John Paul II, had a deep passion for the Black Madonnas.

One of the most striking commonalities in these shrines and statues is that they are predominantly to be found at sites previously associated with pagan worship, in particular, Isis, Demeter, Cybele and Diana and each one of these at some time or other has been depicted with black skin. Their main connection is however, that they were all worshipped as Moon Goddess, with in its Virgin phase, its Mother phase or the Crone or Hag phase, which is also associated with Sophia (Wisdom). Isis appears to be the Goddess that is most often associated with the Magdalene, who as we have seen, is believed to have been a priestess of Isis and had spent time in the Egyptian temples. Isis was also venerated in France and in fact gave her name to Paris (Par Isis).

The Earth Mother has often been portrayed as black throughout history and one of the most important shrines to Mary Magdalene is at Chartres in France, where her shrine surrounds a statue with the name of 'Our Lady Under the Earth', suggestive of the hidden nature of the divine in the Magdalene.

There has also been a suggestion that the black represents the Universal Goddess, the face of the Crone, or the Dark Goddess, associated with hidden wisdom, as in the Sophia.

Relics of St Mary Magdalene bearing blonde wig, at St Baume.

Another strange fact arose during my study of the Black Virgin, and that was that several of these statues bear a scar on the cheek. Not only black but wounded, a fact also noted by Margaret Starbird in her Woman With The Alabaster jar. Appropriate to the Magdalene's plight certainly. The Black Virgin of Czestochowa in Poland bears a deep gash on her cheek. It was this particular shrine of the Black Virgin that was often visited by Pope John Paul II and was the source of his love of the Black Madonna. The Black Madonna at Verviers, Liege, is designated by many as the finest represent-ation of all, one hundred percent black she bears a golden sceptre and crown and more importantly the Sophia's halo of stars, and of course she cradles her infant child who wears the royal crown.

Colour seems to be important in the decoding of religious art forms. Take the issue of clothing for example. In many representations, Mary Magdalene is portrayed as wearing a red cloak, this is in fact an indication of her ecclesiastical status as a high-ranking cleric, examples of which are seen in Botticelli's masterpiece *Mary at the Foot of the Cross* and *Saint Mary Magdalene* by Piero della Francesca. The Roman Church would have none of it, and their subsequent dismissal and association of the Magdalene as a prostitute, along with the wearing of red, may possibly have given rise to our expression 'scarlet woman' to denote a woman of less than savoury repute. So obsessed was the Catholic hierarchy with colour coding, that they decreed that Mary, mother of Jesus, should only be depicted wearing white and blue, so although they pay lip service to the Goddess by the elevation of Mary to Sainthood and venerate her as the Mother of God, they deny her too, the representation of her status as one of the foremost disciples and therefore also a high ranking cleric. No red robes for her.

Solomon's *Song of Songs*, is a moving and beautiful love song which has been associated with the Sacred Marriage of Christ and the Magdalene by modern researchers. In it, in the second canticle, the Bridegroom identifies himself as *'the Rose of Sharon, the lily of the valleys'*, a title often subscribed to Jesus. Later in the verses we find *'I am dark, but lovely'*, from the Bride. Is this another reason for association of the Black Madonna with the Magdalene?

There can be no doubt that the Black Madonnas proved a thorn in the side of the early orthodox church., in particular those appearing in prominent places of Christian worship, such as Chartres Cathedral, and indeed some were removed or repainted into obscurity. Given that the Black Madonna was associated with the Goddess Isis, it is small wonder that as the sacred Feminine was denied by patriarchal religions such as the brand of Christianity we received from Peter and subsequently the Catholic Church, these Black Madonnas found their way into early churches.

Jesus referred to the Magdalene as 'the woman who knew the all', hinting that Mary knew the secret name of God. Further into the past, this knowledge was also attributed to Isis, another link to the Magdalene. The Black Madonna is also linked to Sophia, or Wisdom, who is also black due, according to Lawrence Gardner in his *Bloodline of the Holy Grail* to the fact that she existed in the darkness of Chaos before the Creation.

Another Black Madonna that is steeped in mystery comes from written record. A small boat came ashore in Boulogne i n 633AD. There was no-one aboard, just a statue of the Black Madonna and a copy of the Gospels. The Black Madonna became known as Our Lady of Holy Blood (the Magdalene/ Grail?) and she was instated as such in Boulogne's Notre Dame Cathedral, another reference to the Our Lady being the Magdalene and not Mary, Jesus' mother.

I believe that the Black Madonna symbolises the hidden nature of the Sacred Feminine, her elusiveness, and her return at a time when this earth needs her most, after centuries of the patriarchal loneliness of the Logos, as he yearns for reunion with Sophia, as black or darkness is symbolic of the hidden.

Chapter Ten

The Merovingians and the Holy Bloodline

No contemporary study of Mary Magdalene can ignore the furore that has been caused by the idea that Mary and Jesus produced a child, a daughter called Sarah, and that from this child a holy bloodline was begun and still exists today. I personally do not believe that even if this is so, that it has any relevance today or any effect on the way we should view Christ or the Magdalene, but the controversy is out there and if the Magdalene had children then for her sake we should acknowledge them.

Lawrence Gardner's excellent book *Bloodline of the Holy Grail* is a provocative work of non-fiction, and took years of painstaking research. Gardner's reputation as a historian and royal genealogist is internationally known.

For a base from which to begin, language has once again served us well. The word Desposyni is the term used to refer to the heirs of Jesus and are mentioned in the writings of Eusabius, the 4th century Bishop of Caesarea and Desposyni is the Greek word meaning 'of the master', a special and reverential term to identify any descendent of Jesus' Davidic line.

As previously mentioned, a 'political' marriage between the House of David, and thereby the tribe of Judah and a daughter of the tribe of Benjamin would have brought peace and unity to the people of Israel during the roman occupation, and it is a fact that these two tribes were the closest and most powerful allies and this marriage would have been a beacon of hope for the oppressed.

As such, it would of necessity been kept from all but the most trusted and closest of relatives and friends. If the roman political and military machine had got wind of it, the lives of Jesus and the Magdalene would have been in extreme danger. They would have wanted to avoid such an alliance at all costs, and if, as has been suggested, Mary was pregnant at the time of the crucifixion, it would be even more vital to get her out of the country to protect not only her but the unborn child and the continuance of the bloodline.

We have mentioned the Vine as being used to denote the royal bloodline and the source for this is the Bible itself. The chosen people of God are often referred to as the vine or transplanted vine, and the vine is often ascribed to the feminine, this has led many biblical scholars to agree that it refers specifically to the Davidic line of the tribe of Judah. Jesus himself told us, 'I am the true vine.'

The New Testament is filled with references to Jesus being the Messiah and of the Davidic line alongside passages that refer to him as King. In the triumphal entry to Jerusalem prior to his arrest he is referred to as a king riding a donkey. The significance of the palms is not missed either, as palm fronds are a powerful Jewish symbol. Pilate himself, believed Jesus to be the rightful king, and whilst some attribute the inscription on the cross, Jesus of Nazareth, King of the Jews to sarcasm, it is just possible that Pilate was, in the end, acknowledging Jesus' true heritage. Surely this was reason enough to bring about his arrest and murder, as Palestine was unstable and ready for revolution in need only of a claimant to the throne to spill over into bloody war. Rome could take no chance of an insurrectionist gaining a foothold in Jerusalem. Still more reason to protect his young and pregnant widow after his public execution. Rome would want no focus for the people to rally around.

Returning to the legends and stories of the Magdalene in France, we are told that she arrived in a boat with Martha, Lazarus and an Egyptian child called Sarah. Could this mean that the daughter of Jesus, who we are told was also called Sarah, was born in Egypt? It would make perfect sense for Mary to be whisked away into Egypt in the first instance, as it was known as a safe haven for Jews and closest to the hotbed of unrest in Jerusalem, to travel to France much later, around A.D. 42, making the child approximately twelve years of age. This would tie in with the legend of Sarah, whose name is Hebrew for 'princess' and was about that age.

Could it also be the reason for the Black Madonna connection? Sarah the Egyptian was how she was referred to, but only because she was born in Egypt, but as time passed the dark skinned symbol of the hidden truth of the Magdalene and Grail could easily have blended with the people of the Languedoc assuming that Egyptian meant black skinned.

The work of Lawrence Gardner however, produces a daughter to Jesus and Mary but she is given the name Tamar. She appears in the Bible in Acts as Damaris, the Greek translation of Tamar meaning palm tree, another reference to the Davidic descent.

Scholars and researchers alike are connecting the royal bloodline with the Merovingian kings of France, once again linguistics is providing the key. 'Merovingian' can be supposed to stem from two words mer (Mary) and vin (vine) bringing us to the vine of Mary. That in itself is not enough.

Margaret Starbird, in her brilliant *Woman with the Alabaster Jar* tells of the grave of one of the Merovingian kings, King Childeric I. When his tomb was discovered and opened in 1653 it contained three hundred golden bees. Odd, to say the least. Until that is, we look at the symbolism if these bees in association with the Merovingian line. The bee was in fact the symbol of the Merovingian kings but they were also ancient symbols for Egyptian royalty and of the Goddess of Love. Ever heard of a king bee? The bee population is matriarchal and has a queen at its head. Putting all these together may seem like a leap in the dark but it somehow has the ring of truth in it. The golden bees in the tomb, symbolised King Childeric's descent from the bloodline of Sarah and therefore from the Magdalene and Jesus, making the Merovingian's heirs to the Davidic line. The Merovingian connection turns up again later in the First Crusade, with Godfroi of Lorraine reclaiming Jerusalem, Godfroi was of the Merovingian descent.

Lawrence Gardner's work is extensive and far reaching and beyond the scope of this little book, but is a highly recommended read if a more detailed look into the genealogy of Jesus and his descendants is needed.

Cutting through many generations the Merovingian line gives rise to none other than the bard Taliesin, Lancelot, Galahad and Percival. The Grail family as they became known founded the House of Camulod (Camelot).

Whilst there was precious little in the way of written records during the Dark Ages, much of the history of that time has been reconstructed from documents found in monasteries and archaeological discoveries. Through these records the demise of the Merovingian kings in favour of the Carolingians became known.

Chapter Eleven

Hidden Symbols and the Priory of Sion

I didn't think for a moment that my research for this book would take me into the realm of tarot cards, but they kept appearing from all sorts of different avenues and obviously warranted investigation as to their relevance. They do fall into the thread of connection between the Magdalene and the Holy Grail and into the realms of secrecy and symbolism as a means to perpetuate the Jesus and Mary story in their respective roles as Sacred Male and Female.

My understanding of the origin of the tarot was that they were birthed in Italy but later discovered that there are records of their having been used, and possibly adapted, by the Cathars, possibly in an effort to secrete their teachings into a medium that was unlikely to be burned as heresy. If that was indeed the case, it didn't work, as subsequently, the

Catholic and Protestant churches outlawed tarot and all who used it in an effort to stamp out either heretical teachings or a work of the Devil.

Whilst the Inquisition, surprisingly, did not openly denounce Grail lore as heresy, it did a pretty good job of keeping it under wraps. It isn't amazing then, that devotees such as the Cathars sought to find the use of secret symbols such as in the tarot to distribute and keep alive their 'heresy'. Interestingly, one of the most famous tarot packs is known as the Tarot of Marseilles!

Margaret Starbird's writings on the tarot connection are second to none and provided much insight into the mystery of the Grail/Tarot journey, especially from the standpoint of the Charles VI deck.

The suits of the tarot's minor arcana are Cups (the chalice or grail and symbol for the feminine), Wands or Batons (usually depicted as a sprouting branch, the symbol of the sprouting rod of Joseph of Arimathea), Swords (symbol for the male, and representative of the swords of the Templar Knights) and Pentacles (or plate – another Grail symbol). The Ace of Cups is invariably depicted as an ornate chalice or Grail. It is the eternal symbol of the Sacred Feminine and Masculine in union, the bowl of the chalice representing the womb or Mother and the stem representing the male phallus or Father and the card is invariably associated with a birth or Sacred Marriage.

The major arcana, or trump cards, of the tarot packs are represented by characters that tell a story. We find first of all The Fool, a wandering vagabond type character uncaring as to where his feet fall, and he is perilously close to the edge. A dog is traditionally seeing biting his coat or his heels. This is said to represent the travelling troubadours with their head in the clouds, singing their tales of 'the Lady', whilst the biting dog is representative of the Catholic Church or the Inquisition. The Female Pope would be sure to raise Roman eyebrows, but in the realms of the Cathars and the people of France, folks were comfortable with the idea of women playing important roles within the Church, their Church that is.

The Lovers are said to depict Christ and the Magdalene. Traditional packs show the Lovers with a procession of partying people, these are said to represent the descendants of the Holy Bloodline, the Davidic line, throughout the generations. Margaret Starbird tells us that the original name for this card was 'The Vine'. Curiouser and curiouser.

The Hermit card is said to represent Peter the Hermit, whose enthusiastic preaching contributed to the instigation of the crusades and the subsequent return of Jerusalem to Christianity.

Strength in the tarot pack is most often depicted by a woman overcoming the might of a lion and holding open its jaws. Is it the Lion of Judah? And the symbolism in the woman's strength symbolic of the Magdalene? The High Priestess card usually shows the lady in question with outspread arms, as we often see the Goddess Isis depicted. Is then, another reference to Mary in her role as High Priestess of Isis?

The Tower, dramatically falling into ruin is reminiscent of the MagdalEder, the Watchtower under attack from Rome, whilst The World is obviously a reference to female sovereignty, as the woman holds a sceptre the image of royalty.

It's easy to find hidden symbols in almost any artwork, if you look hard enough, and many would say the symbol is found to fit the story, but there really are far too many 'co-incidences' that fit the Magdalene tale, and the story of the Bloodline. In a climate where a person was put to death with such ease, lips became sealed and the tradition and knowledge, which had to survive, was passed on in subtle means by way of symbols, songs and 'fairy tales'. Working from the standpoint that medieval artists would not incorporate a symbol into a masterpiece without good reason, we must look with different eyes and wonder as to the meaning of the symbols that we find employed in the art of some of the masters.

I had hoped to avoid the controversy surrounding the Priory of Sion, but to continue the search for symbols regarding the alternative church and the artists whose legacy they are, it brings us fairly and squarely back to that enigmatic organisation. So, I will digress for a moment.

The Priory of Sion is at the heart of mystery, conspiracy theories and has been the darling of the debunkers in recent years. It is featured prominently in Dan Brown's *Da Vinci Code* and in *Holy Blood, Holy Grail* by Michael Baigent, Richard Leigh and Henry Lincoln and is a significant factor in whatever was going on in Rennes Le Chateau. It is either a powerful secret society or a magnificent hoax which is why I would rather not dip my toes in this particular water! However, when looking into the significance of the hidden symbology in art we find several names which appear in both spheres.

History or hoax, there are ancient documents held in France in the Bibliotheque Nationale in Paris regarding the Priory of Sion which list geniuses such as Botticelli and Leonardo Da Vinci as Grand Masters. We have already looked at Leonardo's Last Supper with the hidden Magdalene sitting next to Jesus, and there are some that say the leaning away from the central figure of Christ by those on each of his sides forms the letter M – for Mary? Or Magdalene? Botticelli, famous for his big-breasted, round-stomached, ample-bottomed women in his paintings, has been busy at work with several depictions of the Madonna (or is it Mary Magdalene?), in which there are several strange inclusions.

Madonna of the Pomegranate features the infant Jesus with an open pomegranate in his lap. The pomegranate is a well known fertility symbol with its abundance of red seeds, clearly a reference to the fertility of Jesus. In St Mary Magdalene of the Cross, we find the Magdalene prominent in her desolation, hanging on to the cross, but in the background there is an angel holding up a fox by the tail. The fox was a symbol of religious fraud, and there are many medieval depictions of foxes wearing ecclesiastical robes. Is this then, a reference to the deceit of the Roman Church? Margaret Starbird adds to this theory by her allusion to the Song of Songs, where 'little foxes spoil the vineyard of the Bride'. Pretty self explanatory, in my thinking.

Botticelli's *Birth of Venus*, famous for the scallop shell bearing the naked Aphrodite coming out of the sea, bears direct reference to our St Marie De La Mer of Provence. The scallop shell was her symbol and we have already seen her connection to Venus and out of the sea came the Magdalene in southern France. Too many co-incidences for my liking.

The painting by Botticelli that, for me, says everything is *Derelicta*. It features a woman ravaged with grief, her clothing rent asunder as she weeps in front of a closed door. Derelicta means 'abandoned', and the Magdalene torn apart with grief for her Beloved, and firmly shut out of the emerging Church, is most certainly abandoned by the patriarchal society growing under the auspices of Peter.

The Priory of Sion then, if it is history and not hoax, claims both Botticelli and Da Vinci as Grand Masters of their organisation and these two artists have been prolific in incorporating symbology within specific pieces which all point to the same thing, the married status of Jesus and Mary Magdalene as embodiments of the Sacred Male and Female in union, and to the existence of an alternative church whose teachings reflected this in conjunction with a sworn duty to protect the Grail of the Magdalene and the Holy Bloodline.

Derelicta by Botticelli

The Priory was heavily connected with Rennes Le Chateau and prolific study has been occasioned by the mysterious discovery of Berangers Sauniere in the frantic hunt for secret treasure, despite, in my opinion, the treasure being the church itself. The documents regarding the Priory include The Book of Constitutions which tells that the origin of the Order was the Abbey of Our Lady of Mount Sion, in 1099 by none other than our friend Godfroi of Lorraine, our brave crusader and Defender of the Temple.

Subsequent texts within this document is obscure but it can be understood from it that eventually the Priory of Sion undertook the direction of the Knights Templar but they subsequently split away from those noble Knights. The scary part of the story is the revelation that the Order survived down the centuries led by and including amongst its membership those who could affect world affairs and national destinies. Among the list of Grand Masters are, Nicholas Flamel the medieval alchemist, Leonardo Da Vinci, Isaac Newton, Victor Hugo, Claude Debussy eventually to Pierre Plantard St Claire, and yes, it's the same St Claire family of Rosslyn fame.

According to the *Book of Constitutions* the Order assumed the huge responsibility of protecting the Merovingian bloodline until such time as an authentic claimant to the bloodline could be reinstated to the throne of France, which, as we know, never happened.

Much of the information we know of the Priory of Sion has been discounted or proved a hoax, but I wonder how much of the elaborate disinformation was prompted by something very real? By the protected knowledge of the Sacred Bride in Christianity, by the Magdalene.

Chapter Twelve

Women in the Church

It is only within recent years that the Anglican Church has recanted and allowed women to be ordained as priests, although still disavowing their entitlement to the role of Bishop, and the Roman Catholic Church are still adamant that to ordain a woman as priest is against all Christian teachings. I beg to differ, two thousand years ago women were acknowledged by Christ himself as disciples thereby causing scandal amongst the Jewish community who also ascribed to patriarchal domination of religion, and he referred to Mary Magdalene as 'the woman who knew the all' and yet the Bible itself tells us quite clearly that Jesus entrusted the Magdalene alone, with the news of the resurrection, bestowing upon her the role of the Apostle's apostle.

Charges of heresy and blasphemy have been brought to all who have dared to suggest that God has a Goddess, that there is both masculine and feminine in the divine within

Christianity, and although it was Emperor Constantine that performed the act of sacrilege by editing out some of the most important documents which gave credence to the Magdalene and women generally, it was Peter's legacy, adopted by the early church fathers that set the tone for the coming Christian church.

'It is not permitted for a woman to speak in church, nor is it permitted for her to baptise, nor to offer the Eucharist, nor claim for herself a share of masculine function, least of all priestly office.' Quintus Tertullian followed St Paul's distorted doctrine on women and thereby set the seal on women's destiny within the church. If the previous quote held any validity, why then has the Anglican Church overturned this pearl of wisdom and allowed women into the church?

We have seen in previous chapters that Peter, frequently angered by Mary's presence, asked Jesus to silence her because she is, in his eyes, inferior to him. Jesus' response is to rebuke Peter instead (Pistis Sophia), and Jesus designates the Magdalene as the symbol of divine wisdom (Gospel of Phillip).

All of these references were cut by the bishops at the Council of Nicea allowing the patriarchal domination of the church and later by association, the people. The truth about the Magdalene had to be hidden at all costs and by removing all women from any authority or position within the church they sought to deny her rightful place as the wife of Christ and later reduced her to the status of prostitute, however penitent.

Returning to the subject of what did and did not make it into the approved version of the New Testament, one of the initial criteria was that all of the gospels had to be written in the name of the disciples. Whilst Matthew and John were Jesus; disciples, Mark and Luke were not, transgression number one, and two of the gospels written by the apostles Thomas and Phillip got the chop – why? Because they both contained clear references to the true relationship between Jesus and the Magdalene.

It becomes apparent, in light of the discovery of the Nag Hammadi Library, the real criteria behind the Gospel selection was one of fear based sexism denouncing the right of women to hold any status within the clergy.

St Paul seems to want it both ways, denouncing women as worthless and then praising them in later writings to the Romans where he describes Phoebe as a servant of the church and praises both Julia and Priscilla for laying down their necks for the cause.

This frantic effort to remove women's status from the scriptures and the subsequent fear of women that is displayed blatantly within the Roman Church gave rise to the rule of celibacy that has spawned such perversion within its ranks that is now coming to light. Such an unnatural state can only give rise to trouble. Even St Paul, who is renowned for his misogyny, stated that Bishops should be married, because if they could run a family and household, then they could be deemed suitable and capable of running a church. Lawrence Gardner goes even further in this, when he states, The Church was so frightened of women that a rule of celibacy was instituted for its priests; a rule which became a law in 1138 – a rule which persists even today. What really bothered the bishops, however, was not women as such, nor even sexual activity in general terms; it was the prospect of priestly intimacy with women which caused the problem. Why? Because women can become mothers and the very nature of motherhood is a perpetuation of bloodlines – which was a taboo subject which had to be separated from the image of Jesus.' (Bloodline of the Holy Grail)

Chapter Thirteen

The Magdalene Rosary and Mysteries

Ask any group of people about a rosary and the majority will tell you that they are Roman Catholic prayer beads, and whilst this is for the most part true, in recent years the rosary has become a prayer or meditation tool for many other denominations of Christian and non Christian alike. The traditional image is a devout nun with her beads hanging from her tie-belt or kneeling and clicking through the prayers as her mouth moves silently, forming the prayers and devotions traditional to the rosary.

To help us understand the Magdalene Rosary let's first take a look at the traditional beads. The word rosary is derived from the Latin word for a garland of roses for it was the rose that was used as the flower symbol for the Virgin Mary and the rosary is a traditional prayer tool for the intercession of Mary as a mediator between the devotee and their God. It was a clever invention of a group of monks as an aid to those of their brothers who were illiterate and innumerate who were having trouble counting and simultaneously reciting their prayers during devotions. The rosary began life as a simple cord with small and large knots representing the prayers.

After Vatican II, Marian devotions in general became less popular and in particular the rosary beads were used less and less. It is in recent years that we see a resurgence of its popularity helped along by the wearing of designer rosaries by celebrities of screen and football pitch!

Our Magdalene Rosary is a prayer aid to the connection with and devotion to the true Bride of Christ, to the Magdalene. It is used as a tool of intercession of the Magdalene with Christ/God in Man on our behalf and is constructed in a very similar manner to the traditional rosaries. The beads are fashioned from gemstones appropriate to their represent-ations. The chrysocolla bead bears the blue green colour so often associated with the Magdalene, fondly known as Magdalene Blue. Whilst the connection of the Blue and Gold of the Lapis Lazuli share the association of the Magdalene with Egypt. The red jasper is representative of the Blood of Christ as is the carnelian in the lapis and carnelian version, and together they energetically enhance the specific prayers and meditations. Another variation might be rose quartz for the love of the Magdalene and Hematite for the blood of Christ.

The Magdalene Rosary is constructed as seven sets of seven beads (chrysocolla or lapis) separated by a larger or different bead (red jasper or carnelian). Seven is the number of the Divine Feminine, so very appropriate here. There is a medallion or medal, depicting The Magdalene, joining the seven sets of beads from which hang five more beads (a red jasper then a further three chrysocolla beads followed by another red jasper bead) and a Celtic cross (another symbol of the sacred union of male and female divine) or crucifix.

Each bead represents a specific prayer or mantra and each of the seven sections represents the seven Mysteries of the Magdalene in the form of meditations.

The Prayers/ Mantras

The Our Father (said on the red jasper beads).
Our Father Mother which art in Heaven, hallowed be thy name,
Thy kingdom come, thy will be done, on earth as it is in heaven.
Give us this day our daily bread, and forgive us our trespasses as we forgive those that trespass against us. And lead us not into temptation but deliver us from evil, for thine is the kingdom, the power and the glory, forever and ever, Amen.

OR In Aramaic. (Please note that this has been written phonetically to enable the reader to pronounce the Aramaic and in no way is an attempt to write in the original Aramaic or an accepted anglicised version. Speak it as it is written.)

Ar voon duh bash-mire
Nech (the ch sound at the back of the throat) -cardesh Shmok
Tay tay malkoo-tach
Nech-way sevianach eye-carna du bash-mire af ba-ar-ha
Havlan lachma du sunkunan yowmana.
Wash-booklan chow-bain wach-ta-hain eye-carna daf chunan shwokan lach-eye-abain
Wella tachlan lenes-yoona Ella patsan min bisha
Metool dilachay malkoota wa-haila wot-esh-bookta la arlam almeen. Armeyn.

In his brilliant book *Prayers for the Cosmos*, Neil Douglas-Klotz has provided us with a direct translation from the

Aramaic words of Jesus in the Lord's Prayer. His insight into the true meaning of this far reaching teaching is astounding. He has given kind permission to use this translation here in this context and with the Magdalene Rosary.

O Birther! Father- Mother of the Cosmos
Focus your light within us - make it useful.
Create your reign of unity now- Your one desire then acts with ours
As in all light, so in all forms.
Grant what we need each day in bread and insight
Loose the cords of mistakes that bind us,
As we release the strands we hold of others guilt.
Don't let surface things delude us, But free us from what holds us back.
From you is born all ruling will, The power and the life to do,
The song that beautifies all, From age to age it renews.
Truly – power to these statements –
may they be the ground from which all my actions grow.
    Amen.

Here follows another kindred version of the Lord's Prayer that fits in with the ethos of the Magdalene Rosary.

Our Father-Mother who abides in Heaven, Your name be hallowed.
Your sovereignty come, your will be done on Earth as it is in Heaven. Give us what we need each day in food and understanding and forgive our mistakes as we forgive the mistakes of others. And lead us āway from temptation and keep us from all that is evil. For yours is the sovereignty and the power and the glory for eternity. Amen.

And from New Zealand –

The Lord's Prayer
(from the New Zealand Prayer Book)

Eternal Spirit, Earth-maker, Pain-bearer, Life-giver,
Source of all that is and that shall be,
Father and Mother of us all,
Loving God, in whom is heaven:
The hallowing of your name echo through the universe!
The way of your justice be followed by the peoples of the world!
Your heavenly will be done by all created beings!
Your commonwealth of peace and freedom sustain our hope
and come on earth. With the bread we need for today, feed us.
In the hurts we absorb from one another, forgive us.
In times of temptation and test, strengthen us.
From trials too great to endure, spare us.
From the grip of all that is evil, free us.
For you reign in the glory of the power that is love, now and for
ever. Amen

The Hail Mary. (said on the chrysocolla beads).
Hail Mary, Beloved of Christ, The Lord is with you. Blessed
are you who anointed our Lord, who loved you above all other,
return from your exile in darkness to the light of truth. Holy
Magdalene, pray for us now and at the end of days, Amen.

The Glory Be (also said on the red jasper bead).
Glory be to the Father Mother, to the Son and to the Holy
Spirit as it was in the beginning is now and ever shall be,
worlds without end, Amen.

The Hail Magdalene, (said on the Magdalene medal).
Hail Magdalene, your time is come on earth when nations shall hail you and do honour to your name. Take your place in our hearts in balance and harmony with Christ the Saviour, Logos and Sophia restored. Amen

The Magdalene Mysteries

1. Magdalene 'cleansed' in preparation for her work

2. Magdalene anoints Jesus at Bethany.

3. Magdalene at the crucifixion (Matthew 27: 55-56/Mark 15:40)

4. Magdalene at the burial (Matthew 27: 59 – 61 /Mark 15: 46-47)

5. Magdalene at the Resurrection (Matthew 28 :1 -10/Mark

6. Magdalene as Apostle to the Apostles (John 20:16-18 and The Gospel of Mary Magdalene)

7. Magdalene returns from exile.

As each new section of seven beads is reached, one of the above mysteries is meditated upon whilst repeating the necessary prayers or mantra.

The First Mystery is the cleansing or restoring balance to the seven energy centres of the Magdalene's physical form in preparation for her work as consort/Bride who will anoint Jesus as King and Messiah, the Christ. As the beads of this first mystery are chanted visualise the seven chakras or energy centre within your own body becoming open and clear

126

as channels for the Christ/Magdalene consciousness to enter. See each one as a vortex of crystal-clear light.

The Second Mystery, the anointing ceremony, should be meditated upon as a High Initiation Rite. Visualise the Magdalene standing behind the seated Jesus, breathe deeply and see the sacred oil being poured out upon his head and feet. Feel the calm of the acceptance of Jesus of this huge responsibility and the power of the intimacy of this sacred act by his Beloved.

The Third Mystery is the presence of the Magdalene at the foot of the cross as she bears witness to the crucifixion of her Beloved and his tortuous death for the sake of all mankind. Breathe deeply and feel the power and beauty of her witnessing, she knows that her Beloved must die in order to transport himself through Death itself to be resurrected in fulfilment of the prophesies, and in order to show all people that his kingdom conquers even death as he leaves a path of light for all to follow. She must be so sure of his destiny that she can withstand the grief and horror of what she so bravely witnesses.

The Fourth Magdalene Mystery is the Burial of Jesus. She has already begun the preparation of his body for burial and we are told that she accompanies Joseph of Arimathea and Nicodemus to the tomb to further anoint his body. Here we see The Magdalene once more in her role as priestess in her presence as her Beloved begins his journey through Death. How personal her grief and yet how focussed her actions as priestess had to be.

The Fifth Magdalene Mystery and perhaps the most important one is where Mary returns to the garden tomb on the third day, the day after the Passover which has interrupted her ministrations to Jesus' body to find it empty. Here we see her humanity as she grieves openly for the loss of her Beloved and the enormity of his body being taken from the tomb. We see her humanity overtake her training and wisdom as she is ready to believe that his body has been stolen rather than returning to her understanding of what was prophesied and what she understood to be the resurrection. Jesus needs only to speak her name. Imagine the gentleness and compassion in that one spoken word, 'Mary.' She instantly recognises her Beloved and responds with the tender and uniquely intimate name for him, 'Rabounni.' In that instant her training and understanding combine with her human love for the man Jesus as she reaches out to him. This has to be a powerful teaching session as Jesus explains to her the state of his body; that he cannot be clung to because the transition to his light body and ascension has not yet fully taken place. Imagine the depth of her understanding that in this poignant moment of reunion she is able to listen to him as a student rather than a grieving lover and wife.

The Sixth Magdalene Mystery is the commission of the Magdalene by Christ to take the news of his resurrection and the accompanying teachings to the other disciples. Jesus has chosen to appear to Mary first of all and given her the huge responsibility of bringing an understanding of the resurrection to Peter and the others. In this act Christ has ordained Mary as the First Apostle, the Apostle to the Apostles.

The Seventh Magdalene Mystery is perhaps the most personal of all, as we each approach the Magdalene in her role of returning archetype of the feminine Divine in sacred union with the masculine counterpart. As we pray the Magdalene Rosary and acknowledge the first six mysteries we are setting the scene of acceptance by the Universe of her return to her rightful place beside her Beloved.

Each of these mysteries is meditated upon on a certain day of the week. The 1st Mystery is allocated to Wednesday, the 2nd to Thursday, the 3rd Mystery allocated to Friday, the 4th on Saturday, the 5th and 6th on Monday the 7th on Tuesday.

The Magdalene Rosary can be easily made using the recommended beads or any other that resonate as appropriate.

* * * *

A Novena For the Magdalene

What is a novena? It is a series of prayers and/or meditations combined with the reading of uplifting passages from scripture or other sources that take place over nine hours, days or weeks addressed to a particular Goddess, Saint or patron.

Day 1

Prayer: *O Magdalene, you were cleansed by Jesus to prepare you for your work and life with Him. How you felt at that time we can only imagine. We know that you were His beloved and that your love for Him was precious. Thank you, for that love and for the love that you give to all those who also live in the Christ consciousness. Amen*

Reading: Mark 16:9

Meditation: Think what it must have been like in those days to be a woman alone. It was a man's world and women were valued only for their dowries or their domestic work. Preaching and listening to the gospels was only for the men.

Mary already had an unfounded bad reputation and she knew that to become a disciple and follower of Christ she was going to face much opposition. Whilst Jesus was careful not to break any Judaic Laws of the day, he had no care for the exclusion of women from spiritual matters and recognised in Mary one who understood the soul, its make-up and mechanics, and how it progressed to ascension. He recognised the true capacity for love in her heart and took her to his own heart as He prepared her for the work that lay ahead of her.

Day 2

Prayer:

O Magdalene, how painful it must have been for you to see your brother Lazarus die. You knew that had Jesus been there he would have healed him and he would not have known the realms of death. When the Lord arrived, you remained indoors until he sent for you in the tradition of a husband returning to his home. And when he saw your distress, he too wept. How your faith was rewarded when you saw Lazarus emerge from the tomb, whole again at the word of Jesus. Help us also to have faith that Jesus will be there for us when the time is right and to trust his judgement in all matters. Amen

Reading: John 11:1- 43

Meditation: Imagine how Mary must have felt. She knew that word had been sent to Jesus that her brother Lazarus was ill and feared to be close to death and yet Jesus did not come in time to save him. She didn't cry or question him like her sister Martha, she knew that Jesus would do what was right and her faith was rewarded when her brother was restored to life after being in the tomb for four days. Are we quick to question the Lord's judgement in matters that we have put into his hands? Perhaps Mary's example could help us accept His responses.

Day 3

Prayer:

O Mary, you will always be remembered with your alabaster jar of nard which you used to anoint our Lord Jesus, Christ and King. You understood what it meant on that day when you poured the nard out on His head and feet and as you wiped His feet with your hair and you understood your role as the sacred Bride to the sacrificial Bridegroom. How your heart must have ached knowing that you would soon lose your beloved by your very act of love and recognition. Help us to remain true to our calling even when we know that it will cost us dearly. Amen.

Reading: John 12:1-11(NIV)

Meditation: How often are we asked to do something that we know is going to cost us dearly in love or friendship and how often do we find a reason not to do it because of that? Mary knew that in anointing Jesus she was helping him to fulfil the prophesies in that he would be the 'Christos' the 'anointed one', she also realised that in keeping with other traditions the wife of the Bridegroom to be sacrificed would be the one to prepare him by anointing him with sacred oils and unguents and recognised what else was being played out here. She knew that this act was effectively putting the seal on Jesus' role as being the Bridegroom sacrifice for the good of his people. Yet she carried out her task even though her heart must have been breaking, especially as it was obvious that no-one else realised the significance of what was taking place.

Day 4

Prayer:

O Magdalene, how your heart must have been breaking as you watched your beloved suffer on the cross for all of our sins. How you must have wanted it all to go away and how easy it would have been for you to have been bitter at your loss for our sakes. Yet you showed your love for us as He had taught all the disciples and in your grief you never left His side. Help us to be like you and show His kind of love for all mankind even as we suffer loss. Amen

Reading:

John 19:1 -25

Meditation:

Mary has not only seen her beloved condemned to death on the cross by an angry mob, she knows it is for the sake of that very same angry mod that he is to die. How easy it would be for her to turn what she had learned from Him into a hatred for those that had brought him to his death and yet she became the First Apostle, and carried on His teachings. Could we, in all honesty, remain true to our beliefs in the face of such apparent injustice?

Day 5

Prayer: *O Mary, beloved of Jesus, you saw Him laid in the tomb yet could not carry out your sacred task of anointing his precious body as the Sabbath approached. The hours of the night must have seemed like days, as you held vigil alone and in patience. Grant us the patience to wait in silence when we know that nothing can be done in any situation. Amen*

Reading: Mark 5 : 42 – 47

Meditation: Her beloved was dead. All she could do for him now was prepare his body by anointing it with sacred oils that would help his soul pass through the various stages of death. But time was against her and she couldn't violate the Sabbath so she had to sit in silent vigil as the hours passed. How helpless she must have felt and how interminable the day must have seemed. She accompanied Joseph to the tomb to see where his body was laid and had to return home and wait for the time to pass. How many of us could turn aside from a loved one to keep holy the Sabbath day? Mary did.

Day 6

Prayer: *Beloved Magdalene, we can only guess at the fear that must have engulfed you at the tomb on the Monday morning when you found it empty and the Lord's body gone from sight. The others had left you not understanding that Jesus had to rise from the tomb to fulfil the scriptures but in your grief you remained there. And he came to you. In that glorious moment you alone were the witness to the risen Christ. You became the*

Apostle to the Apostles although unrecognised
and dismissed by the others. Help all nations to
see you as you should be seen, as Jesus saw you,
as The Magdalene. Amen

Reading: Mark 16:9-11

Meditation: As if her grief was not enough, Mary finds her beloved's tomb empty. She remains in the garden weeping and then from nowhere, Jesus appears to her. He speaks her name and in that instant nothing else mattered. She wanted to touch him, to feel him close to her again but here we have a lesson in the progress of the soul after death as Jesus tells her that she mustn't cling to him as he still has to ascend. Then, in a defining moment, he commissions her as the First Apostle, the Apostle to the Apostles, to take her advanced knowledge and her witness to the resurrection to the others. He set her above Peter and all the other disciples by choosing to appear to her first. Here begins the betrayal of the Magdalene as Peter and the others dismiss her and put her aside in disbelief needing to see for themselves the risen Christ.

Day 7
Prayer: *O Holy Magdalene, you who carried the deeper*
spiritual truths taught by Jesus, were sidelined
and ignored by the male disciples who scorned
you without Christ's presence to protect you. We
have come to see that you were threatened for
your love of the saviour and because of his great
love for you. We pray that now in these more
enlightened days that your truth will be heard

*again and those precious teachings entrusted
into your gentle care will be in everyone's heart.
Amen*

Reading: Pistis Sophia – Book Two

Meditation: Here we begin to see more clearly the real
tensions between Mary and Peter and some of
the other male apostles and the culture of the
day at odds with the true nature of Jesus'
teachings. Mary actually gives voice to her
fears about Peter to Jesus. She feels threatened physically and is fearful of Peter and his
hot temper and obvious hostility to women in
ministry as well as his jealousy of Jesus' love
for the Magdalene. This exchange also shows
us how fragile her safety was seemingly only
protected whilst Jesus was around. Indeed we
see more clearly the side of Peter's nature that
have given rise to some of the more misogynistic traits of the Roman Catholic Church, as
he reveals himself to be a bully with little or no
understanding of the real teachings of Christ.
How can we ensure that this isn't perpetuated
any further? We must understand that we are
all gifted differently and each is a cherished
person in their own right. There is no room for
jealousy and suspicion in the state of our world
today. It is time for the Magdalene's voice to be
heard.

Day 8
Prayer: *Mary, you have shown us the nature of spirit
and how our souls can aspire to ascend in the
way that Jesus ascended. As our world becomes
more and more dense, consumed by*

materialism and matter, help us to understand the interconnection between our souls and our bodies and the everlasting nature of spirit. Grant us your wisdom to perceive what is required to enable our souls to ascend. Amen

Reading: The Gospel Of Mary Magdalene

Meditation: The Gospel of Mary is different from the majority of the Gnostic Gospels in that it is easily understood and beautiful in its language. Mary passes on her knowledge of the nature of the soul and how it works in connection with our bodies and minds. In this context she is the forerunner of our understanding of holistic medicine in that she teaches that the body mind and soul are interlinked and respond to each other in ways that are only now becoming recognised. She passes on the teachings of Christ about the nature of matter and how it decomposes but the nature of soul is immutable and lives on. Contemplate how everything returns to its source. Matter to matter, spirit to spirit.

Day 9
Prayer: *O my Magdalene, Jesus held you in such high esteem and loved you more than all the others. Your heart was filled with love for him, your mind was filled with understanding of his teachings, your soul was filled with his light. Help us to transcend the doubts, fears and material obsessions we have to enable us to be more like you. You were blessed with an understanding of the mysteries grant us too an understanding of the soul's mysteries.*

Reading:	Pistis Sophia – Book 1
Meditation:	Think about the words of Jesus in this text. He says: *'Mary, thou blessed one, whom I will perfect in all mysteries of those of the height, discourse in openness, thou, whose heart is raised to the kingdom of heaven more than all my brethren.'* They speak for themselves, of Christ's great love and respect for Mary's advanced soul. Christ says later in the same manuscript, *'Where I shall be, there will also be my twelve ministers. But Mary Magdalene and John, the virgin, will tower over all my disciples and over all men who shall receive the mysteries. And they will be on my right and on my left. And I am they, and they are I.'* It is here we find reference to the division of Jesus' teachings into two churches. The Roman Catholic Church, based on Peter's words and doctrines, complete with its denigration of women in the church and the Johanine Church, founded by Mary and John, based on the more advanced and almost secret teachings of the Saviour, for those who 'had ears to hear'. In other words for those whose souls and wisdom was advanced enough in those days to comprehend. We are fortunate now to be living in a time of enlightenment and education and we can all aspire to the higher teachings of Christ, if we simply open our hearts and minds to the possibilities.

* * * *

Sacred Anointing Oils

As we have already seen from the canonical gospels, the Gnostic gospels and portrayed in art, the Magdalene was skilled in the use of sacred essential oils, becoming widely known as the woman who anointed Christ with precious nard, spikenard as we know it. In France the amygdala gland, which is part of our brain which responds to sense of smell, is said to have been named after the Magdalene. This gland is part of our limbic system, the part of us which can activate our higher spiritual centres. A legacy of the Magdalene then, is our understanding of aromatherapy and a dawning of a 're-appreciation' of the nature and healing energies within essential oils when used in massage or bathing or as a perfume.

The following oil blends have been channelled by ministers of The Church of Christ and Mary Magdalene, specifically for use prior and during meditations and services for the Christ Consciousness, The Magdalene, and the Sacred Union.

Caution! These are neat essential oils and should be used with care; Frankincense and Cypress should not be used during pregnancy. If in doubt, please consult a qualified aromatherapist or medical professional before use. Use I drop only of the blend in 5 drops of olive oil.

The Magdalene Oil

Rose Absolute	10 drops
Geranium	7 drops
Palma Rosa	5 drops
Spikenard	3 drops
Cypress	2 drops

Use this oil blend to access the higher consciousness and the Divine Feminine, in meditation or ritual.

Christ Consciousness Oil

Frankincense	7 drops
Spikenard	5 drops
Myrrh	5 drops
Sandalwood	3 drops

This powerful blend gives access to the Christ Consciousness, the moving power in our time, when compassion and harmony within humanity will once again come from the Divine Masculine principle in union with his bride.

Sacred Union Oil

Frankincense	7 drops
Myrrh	5 drops
Rose Absolute	7 drops
Spikenard	5 drops

This blend of oils moves us forward to the realm of sacred union, both spiritual and sexual. The true alchemy of the spirit can come about when accessing the sacred union of the feminine and Masculine Divine in union.

Anointing the third eye with any one of these oil blends prior to meditation or ceremonial will help access the higher realms of spirit required to commune with the Divine in all its aspects, Male, Female and in Sacred Unity.

* * * *

The Feast of Mary Magdalene - July 22nd

Although, as we have seen, the people of Provence celebrate the life of Mary Magdalene on the day that she came ashore near Marseilles, the Roman catholic Church, having designated her 'Saint' Mary Magdalene, have allocated July 22nd as her Feast Day. Throughout Europe many churches, especially those bearing her name, are alight with candles and incense on this day.

The Magdalene is so much more than a patron saint, she embodies, in human form, the Sacred Feminine, the Sophia to Christ's Logos and as such deserves recognition and celebration both within the orthodox churches and from the Gnostic point of view.

Devotion to the Magdalene is widespread and becoming more so with each passing day, and so I have included a form of celebration that I believe to be suitable for all.

The Song of Songs of the Old Testament has become associated with the Magdalene and Christ as it tells of the sacred marriage of the Bride and Bridegroom. Modern theologians have agreed that it illustrates the heiros gamos or sacred marriage and was frequently heard in Jesus' Palestine. Whilst the Jewish hierarchy believed its was a metaphor for God's love of his people Israel, and as such was holy property it became increasingly popular in secular surroundings, in banquet halls and in the streets. What then is the basis for its connection with Jesus?

Canticle 2 states specifically *I am the Rose of Sharon and the lily of the valleys*' another name given to Christ. It continues *'As the lily among thorns, so is my love among the daughters.'* The Magdalene has long been associated with the lily, and a lily is often seen in portraits of her.

Today, there are numerous websites, churches and organisations dedicated to the Magdalene, even an Order of Mary Magdalene, and our own church is named The Church of Christ and Mary Magdalene, as awareness grows daily of the need for recognition of the sacred masculine and feminine to be in balance in the patriarchal form of Christianity. The Feast of Mary Magdalene is an ideal opportunity for restoring the lost bride to her rightful position.

A Prayer to the Magdalene
Our Lady Magdalene, mystery and light are found in you
Whole and complete is your love.
Sophia to the Logos, your mysteries are infinite,
Apostle to Apostles, Teacher of Teachers,
Sacred Bride in Exile, your titles are many.
But to us you will always be
Blessed Amongst Women.
Grant me your wisdom, your strength
and your grace, which lights up the world.
Holy Magdalene, pray for us. Amen.

For me, the most appropriate hymn or song of praise for the Magdalene, has to be In The Garden. The words are evocative of that first witness of the resurrection by Mary the beloved of Jesus, of her unwillingness to leave him and go to the others and of his own grief as she parts from him. It is an oft enjoyed hymn in our own church and it seems more than appropriate on this occasion of her Feast day.

In The Garden
I come to the garden alone, While the dew is still on the roses
And the voice I hear, falling on my ear, The Son of God discloses.
And He walks with me And He talks with me
And He tells me I am His own
And the joy we share as we tarry there None other has ever known
He speaks and the sound of His voice Is so sweet the birds hush their singing

And the melody that He gave to me Within my heart is ringing
And He walks with me And He talks with me
And He tells me I am His own
And the joy we share as we tarry there None other has ever known

I'd stay in the garden with Him 'Tho the night around me be falling
But He bids me go; through the voice of woe His voice to me is calling
And He walks with me And He talks with me
And He tells me I am His own
And the joy we share as we tarry there None other has ever known

* * * *

Chapter Fourteen

The Magdalene Speaks

My name is Mariam, although you probably know me better as Mary Magdalene. My story is known to you through the gospels written so long ago, although through fear and tradition it has been twisted until, to most people I am nothing more than a repentant whore. My Yeshua is so sad about that, as He is about many things that are done in His name.

I have waited throughout the centuries for enlightenment to come to the people of this Earth and hoped and longed for the day when my truth will be told and understood and my voice heard once more, when I am accepted for what I am and not what men would have me be. For the earthly representative of the Sacred Feminine.

But then, the teachings and yearning for people to live in love that were so central to my Beloved's mission have also been subjected to misinterpretation, mistranslation and even edited out of the scriptures altogether, some of it accidental, some not so, to suit the patriarchal whims of men living in fear of the truth. The truth that is so simple and yet apparently so difficult for men to live by, that all humanity should live in, and live by, love. It is the truth that will set mankind free.

Now at the time when the future of the Earth and of humanity is so fragile there is an awakening, a quickening, and an awareness that unconditional and pure love is essential to the survival of all. I see the obscenity of starvation and famine contrasted with great wealth, war in almost every nation, and the desire for material possession taking centre stage. Brother takes up arms against brother, nation against nation. This is as revealed by Yeshua (Yeshua is the Aramaic name of Jesus) when we walked the shores of Galilee together and later to John on the island of Patmos. Revelations and awareness are blossoming now for you all, you have even given it a name – the Christ Consciousness.

All things must change, old beliefs and barriers must be broken down and pass away for the Kingdom to be birthed right here on the earth. My part in that story is tiny, compared to that of Yeshua, my Beloved, but my own truth is slowly becoming known and revealed to many as the gospel written in my name is known amongst men. It began like this.

I am familiar with the voice of my own Soul. I know its tones, its nuances and accents, its depths and its heights. Yet when Soul spoke to me that morning, it was with a voice that was demanding and urgent and without precedent.

"Go to the well,' it said, 'Draw from it your purpose. The one who will meet you there will be your guide and your Teacher and you will show to Him the Humanity in the sacred union.

Your wisdom will bloom and you will become the Sophia to the Logos.'

It was in the burning heat of midday that I first saw Him approach the well. We came from opposite directions, He from the East, and I from the West. As he neared the well his image became blurred as in a mirage. The searing light of the sun mingled with his blinding radiance and played tricks with my eyes. I recognised him immediately, he was a frequent visitor to my home in Bethany, my family gave support to his mission and I had fallen into his eyes on many an occasion. My brother Lazarus had never mentioned a marriage although a daughter of a family such as ours had a duty to marry well, if not politically. I am of the Tribe of Benjamin and an alliance with the House of David of the Tribe of Judah could bring a return of the rightful King to the throne of Israel. There were many prophesies surrounding such an event and a Messiah was well overdue, though the Zealot's had redemption of a different kind in mind. But, as my heart leapt at the sight of him, as His dark eyes drew mine into him, none of that was important,

I had stood amongst the crowds listening to Him on the shores of Lake Galilee and at His feet very recently when He had visited my home and dined with Lazarus, my brother. It was Yeshua, the one they called The Nazarene.

I looked into His eyes and was immediately held transfixed as in them I saw the Son of God, the Son of Humanity, The Soul of Souls, and the Oneness of All That Is. My own eyes filled with tears and my heart expanded until I believed it would burst. I feared that I would lose consciousness from the power of the love that emanated from Him.

I fell to my knees in His presence and reached out to Him. He took my hands in His and I was found.

'Mary,' He said, and He made my name sound like a prayer.

'Rabbouni', I whispered.

I don't know how much time passed, it could have been an eternity or just a heartbeat but in that space and time I felt my Soul touch His and my entire being was enveloped in His aura. When he released me he laid His hand on the crown of my head and with His other hand He gently touched the centre of my forehead. I knew of the energy centres in the body, they were known to me as the Seven Portals, and I was aware of a huge shift in the energy within my body as each of the portals was cleared and aligned. As the shift took place I saw images that represented the unwholesome aspects associated with each centre and felt the emotions of lust, greed, envy, gluttony and jealousy enter and leave my being with such a force as to make me cry out in anguish. Yeshua had cast out my seven 'demons' and I stood before him cleansed.

His face showed no emotion as He waited for me to speak first.

I searched for words that would tell him of the healing I had received, of the openness and expanse in my heart centre, but no words were adequate and I felt a little foolish.

He smiled, first from His eyes then his mouth, 'Mary, you are prepared now. God has chosen you for important work. '

Thoughts blew through my head like dust on the desert wind. Although Jewish, I had served as a Priestess of Isis, a temple servant. I had heard Yeshua speak of his God but I had been a handmaid of Lady Isis for many years, even though the others in my family were loyal to the God of Abraham. I didn't know how this could be. Surely His God would not look kindly on one that had not come to Him in worship, one who had knelt before what He called a pagan Goddess seeking the feminine in the divine. I was troubled.

He knew my thoughts. 'You have knowledge of the Soul, Mary; you know the gateways that it must pass through in what is called Death. You have sacred knowledge of anointing oils and practices. I must soon be anointed as the Christ, the Messiah. You are high in the tribe of Benjamin and I am of the house of David. It is for you to prepare me for my journey. My time here is short, soon I will be taken to a place of Death and to fulfil the scriptures, I will die on a cross, be buried and rise again on the third day. I will return to my people and I will then go back to my heavenly parent.'

'Ascension?' I asked.

He nodded, 'I will ascend to my Father-Mother in heaven until the day comes for my return to this world.'

I knew the theory of the Soul's ascension process but I had no experience or intimate understanding of it. He was right, I knew of the sacred practices and rituals of anointing and of preparing a Soul for its journey through the gateways, but I was not ready for this. Instinctively I knew His words were true and now I also knew that He truly was the Son of God. But what of my beloved Isis?

Again He knew what was in my head. 'Mary, sit with me while I explain to you the nature of God.'

The sun was fading into the horizon when he finished talking. He explained how God, was the only God, the One God, who was eternal, ever present, and all encompassing. He called God 'Father', 'Abba' in our tongue, but how, in truth, God is neither male nor female but both, Mother and Father, All. The pagan Gods and Goddesses were mere shades of the One God, created by man to explain their own creation. He showed me

147

how my service to Isis had prepared me for acceptance of the female aspect of the One God, the Goddess part of God that could not be separated from the Oneness, from All That Is.

I knew that from that moment onwards, my life would be forever changed. I could no longer return to the temple; instead my footsteps would shadow His until His journey was over. I felt the tug at my heart centre when I realised just how the end would leave me. Bereft and mourning for my love, for the one who would only return at the end of days. Did I want that?

I had long since put away thoughts of marriage, content instead to live my life in temple service. I knew that people called me a harlot, a prostitute of the temple, but they were wrong. My duties at the temple were not those of a sacred whore, though of those there were many, but my work was that of attending the sick and the dying and preparing their Souls for the journey across the abyss. I stood watch over the bodies as the Souls journeyed and passed through the gateways and the trials of the different levels of existence until they finally passed into what I now perceived as Yeshua's heaven, His Kingdom. I felt unworthy and yet He quite clearly expected me to accept the enormity of what He was proposing. I tried to pray to Isis, but the words lay impotent and unspoken. Instead I felt a connection of spirit with an energy force that was so powerful it almost stopped my heart from beating, my blood from flowing in my veins. As I looked at Yeshua, His radiance blinded me and everything was engulfed in his light, as though the midday sun had held my gaze, and when He spoke His voice held the Universe in its embrace.

'Mary, do not doubt. You are indeed the one. My chosen one'

For the second time I fell to my knees, this time with my head bowed. My voice shook as all I could utter was, 'God. My God.'

The days that followed were as a dream. I returned to Bethany changed forever by my visit to the well from which I had drawn the living water. Night followed day in a succession of confusion and joy and I began to wonder if it had all been a dream as each day I went wherever He was and met the love in his eyes with a smile. He taught me much, and although it vexed Peter and some of the others, he continued to share deep truths with me whenever we could be alone. Sometimes John was there too, only he among the others understood the advanced ideas and teachings that Yeshua brought to us.

News came of the death of the Baptist and I knew He would be in grief. I sought Him out in a precious moment when we could be alone together. These times were few and far between, Peter saw to that.

'Mary.' His voice was soft and his eyes penetrated me as they always did. 'You heard then?'

I nodded. 'He was important to you', I said.

Yeshua nodded and a silent tear appeared on his lean cheek. I wanted to comfort Him but knew not how to. He understood my confusion.

'I am the Son of God, Mary, but I am present in the body of a man. I came from my Father to know the trials and the emotions of men and I grieve for John. He was my cousin and my prophet and he was dear to me.'

In that moment I knew that I loved Him with everything that was in me and of me. I loved Him as the Messiah, the Son of God, but I also saw and loved the man in him. I reached out and caught the tear as it travelled down His face. I felt His anguish then and was shocked at the depths of His grief. This man who was to be called the Lamb of God, who had healed many of terrible diseases just by the mere touch of His hand, who had healed some just by the very thought and had even brought others back from the dead, even He could not assuage His own grief. In that instant I knew that I was to be His disciple, His lover, His friend; that I would travel with Him wherever I could, that my household would be His household. I knew also, that He loved me too. He loved all mankind with an unconditional love that would one day be the saving grace of this world, but He loved me then, in that moment, as a woman. The Son of Humanity, Word made flesh, loved me as I loved Him. Whatever would become of me mattered nothing from then on, all was at peace in my Soul and I knew God.

He took my hands in His and, as always, at His touch my aura sparked with the charge of His high frequency energy. He knelt and pulled me to the floor with Him, facing each other and palm to palm. Without warning my conscious mind shifted and our hands traced a common pathway through the air, travelling in a direction governed not by the mind but by the spirit. The pain and expansion in my heart centre exploded into a crescendo of light as I realised that my Soul was merging at some level with His. When at last our hands were still, I told Him that I knew of this as the Dance of the Souls, although it was a dance that I had never experienced.

Later as we lay together our auras merged and we were within one energy field, our seven portals locked together as if by iron bars, we truly were one.

Amongst the many Priestesses at the temple there were those who were trained in sexual alchemy, skilled in the art of connecting to the Divine through ecstasy and this was one of their practices. I remembered the voice of Soul on that first day and how it had spoken of sharing with Yeshua the art of sacred union. I remembered the ancient saying 'As above so below.' and realised the truth in the teachings that to return to God we all must learn to balance the male and female Divine within ourselves. In sacred union we became one with the Divine.

Yeshua had many disciples, but the twelve were always with Him. We were based at Capernaum but travelled far each and every day, sleeping rough sometimes in the cold of the night in the desert. At the pool in Bethesda I saw him talking with a man who had been an invalid for thirty-eight years. He told the man to take up his bed and walk. And just by the power of these very words, the man did walk. I heard some Jews rebuke the man for carrying his bed on the Sabbath and wondered at their small mindedness. I didn't know then that this would be only the first of the fierce opposition that Yeshua would meet from the Pharisees, even to the Sanhedrin, as they became more and more imprisoned by the Law and not set free by it as was the intention. My Beloved would seek to teach them in gentle ways, but they would not listen and they would not see. Deaf and blind and refusing to be healed.

Even amongst the others there was dissension, as daily Peter's hostility to me increased and became open, even in front of Yeshua. He always defended me and that in itself aggravated Peter. I didn't want to think about what would happen to me once His prophesies were complete and I was alone. I knew that Peter would lose no time in ensuring that it was he and not I that would lead the others if he had his way. It wasn't leadership for its own sake that was important, but leadership in the spirit and understanding of the deeper spiritual truths that Yeshua had shared. There would come a time when the soul's ascension was paramount and without true knowledge many would miss out o the opportunity. I prayed that when that time comes, some at least will have searched long and hard enough and my voice may be heard.

Day after day Yeshua taught His message of love and of the coming of the Kingdom of God. We walked for mile after dusty mile as He asked all to love one another and to have hope in

151

the Kingdom of Heaven. He gave hope to many thousands and one day at the end of the afternoon when he had been teaching a great crowd, he fed them all from just a few loaves and fishes, and none went hungry. Such was His greatness and His concern for all.

I'm sure He knew of the way that Peter looked at me for he had made it plain that he thought that a woman's place was not at the side of the Lord but in the kitchens or out in the fields. He certainly didn't like it when I sat with them to listen to His teachings. Women, in his way of thinking, could not be disciples. I tried hard not to antagonise him but Peter needed no prompting. He tried to dismiss me whenever he could or belittle me whenever possible. I said nothing; Yeshua had enough to think about without the pettiness of Peter's insecurity and jealousy.

As days became weeks my Lord, my Yeshua, healed many, the lame, the leper, the blind, the possessed; but instead of praise and acceptance, he met with more and more opposition from the Pharisees. Their Law was inflexible and they refused to believe that here, truly, was the Messiah, the Son of God even when they saw with their own eyes, Yeshua restore life to the dead. When He spoke of forgiving people's sins, it brought things to a head and they demanded that he retract, as their fear of displacement of their power grew in proportion to their position and false pride.

Yeshua continued with His mission and taught more and more people about the Kingdom of His Father. He taught that love and repentance was the key to forgiveness and entry into that Kingdom and He taught those with limited understanding by telling stories or parables that they could easily relate to.

I was at home, at Bethany, when my brother Lazarus fell ill. It happened so quickly and we feared that he would die. I sent a message to Yeshua, asking that He come, knowing that He would heal Lazarus and restore him to us. Days went by and Lazarus slipped away from us. I knew that the news of his death had reached Yeshua and that he would come, even though he was too late. Martha went out to meet Him and I heard her grief give way to rebuke at His letting our Lazarus die. I went to Him then too.

'He would not have died if you had been here,' I wept.

I could see how He was moved by my tears as his own shed tears of grief in keeping with my own. 'Take me to where he is,' He said.

He followed me to the tomb and told some of the mourners to take away the stone. I saw Him pray to His Father- Mother and then in wonder I saw Him raise his arms and he called out, 'Lazarus! Come out!'

Everyone was silent as we waited for what seemed an age. Then as if from the womb and not the tomb, Lazarus stood before us, alive and healthy, a living man dressed in grave clothes.

I saw the faith of many turn to Yeshua and His Father God that day but some of the witnesses went to the Pharisees and they called a meeting with the Sanhedrin and from that day on they plotted to take His life rather than lose their own status and power. My beloved, was a threat to their positions and they were not about to take it lying down.

It was drawing close to the Passover and we were at dinner at Bethany. Before dinner He came to me and drew me aside.

'It is to be tonight, Mary. You are ready?'

Although prepared for this moment, I still felt my heart leap. This would be the beginning of the end, I knew it. Tonight would seal the fate of my beloved.

I nodded at Him, unable to speak of my dread. I had no need, He knew my Soul.

I sat at his feet, listening to His words, devouring them, burning them into my heart. Martha came from the kitchen then, hot and flustered. She complained to Him that I sat at his feet instead of helping her with the meal. I knew it wasn't jealousy with Martha but I also knew that she did not see me as a disciple. Peter's influence reached even to my own sister. I stood to go and help her, but He motioned for me to be seated again.

'Martha, you are worried about too many things. Mary has chosen the better part and it shall not be taken away from her.' he said simply. 'Leave her here.'

I was torn then, I wanted to remain as close to Him as I could but I also wanted to help Martha. I knew also that soon He would be gone from us. He had told of His own death many times; Peter and the others denied it, but I knew the truth of His words. I stayed with Him whilst Martha served dinner, feeling that I had let her down but knowing that I had done the right thing. She knew nothing of what was about to happen.

As everyone reclined at the table, content from Martha's wonderful cooking, they listened to Yeshua. His eyes made contact with mine and I knew what lay in his heart and in His gaze. I rose and collected from my closet the alabaster jar containing the purest nard, a whole pound of it. The jar was heavy and the fragrance filled my room before my shaking hands had even broken the seal.

I took my place behind Him and everyone fell silent. In keeping with the traditions, I broke the seal of the jar and poured the nard onto my beloved's head and then onto His feet. I wiped the oil from his skin with my hair and washed it with my tears. It was done; he was anointed in fulfilment of the scriptures. He was the Christ. The Anointed One and Messiah.

People were speaking all at once; I could hear several above the others. Peter was complaining yet again about me, and not one of them realised the real significance of what had just taken place, but it was Judas' voice that was the loudest, bemoaning my use of such an expensive unguent when the money could have been given to the poor instead. I wanted to explain myself, but had no need as my Beloved was swift to my defence.

Yeshua spoke and all were silenced. 'Leave her alone. It was intended that she save this perfume to prepare me for burial. You will always have the poor, but you will not always have me. Wherever the gospel is told, all over the world, this will be told in remembrance of her.' He was asking them to acknowledge the ceremony they had just witnessed, the ritual marriage of the Sacred Bride and Bridegroom of the scriptures. He wanted them to tell all of our sacred marriage but they were so taken up with Judas' criticism that the true significance of our act eluded them.

No-one dared to argue with Him although some were obviously discontented when the party broke up and still none had realised that they had been witness to the anointing of Christ the King. Not even I wanted to accept that when Passover came, the world would be forever changed.

The following day I was amazed to see people lining the streets, all of them excited and waving palm fronds. I stopped and asked one of them what the cause of all the excitement was.

'Yeshua of Nazareth is coming', the man said 'We are here to greet Him who comes in the name of the Lord'.

This would not please the Pharisees who were already nervous at His popularity and at how many people were following Him, they saw it as eroding their own authority. It would mean trouble. I returned to the house where Yeshua was preparing to leave, to warn him. He was asking Lazarus to procure a donkey for him.

'I will ride into Jerusalem on this donkey, and the prophesies will be fulfilled. It is written Do not be afraid O Daughter of Zion; see, your king is coming, seated on a donkey.'

The crowds were shouting 'Hosanna! Blessed is He that comes in the name of the Lord! Blessed is the King of Israel!' My unease grew as I saw groups of Pharisees witnessing his triumphal entry and talking together in hushed voices, but said nothing to my beloved.

Yeshua told us all then that he was about to die, that He would be condemned to a harsh death and it was close. In the upper room we met for the Passover Feast and I sat at his side when my Beloved initiated what was to become The Eucharist in His memory. He stunned all into silence momentarily as he told us that one of us present would betray him and lead the Pharisees to arrest him. Peter, as usual protested loudly. My Beloved leaned to him and told him that before the cock would crow, he too would betray him, by denying that he knew him, not just once but three times. Peter would not accept that and fell into a black mood, poor Peter, who loved my Yeshua so desperately and wanted with all his heart to understand his teachings but just could not get past the patriarchal heritage that he carried like a burdensome yoke.

I knew of the things that my Beloved spoke of, for He had already told me in the quiet of the night. My heart ached for

Him as there was nothing I could say that would give Him ease, I wanted to take His burden away, but only His Father could do that and that would not come to pass because His destiny was long since written. Which one, I wondered? Which one would forfeit the life of one so great? And for what?

He comforted me as I wept for Him. 'Save your tears for them, Mary. Comfort them, for I know they do not understand as you do. They will be lost; believing that all else is lost. I know that you understand that in my end is my beginning. You have an understanding and a love that is so dear to me.'

'Peter will keep them together,' I said through my tears.

'Peter. Ah yes, but first he will deny my very existence no less than three times. He will be afraid for his own life, as will the others. But you, Mary, you, I know will be there by my side. It will help the man in me to fulfil the work of the Word.'

'Rabbouni', was all I could say. There was nothing to which I could give voice that would ease the pain within me or Him. I could not bear to go with Him to Gethsemane and I knew he wanted me far from his agony in that cursed garden. I would not have withstood the torment and anguish that would rack through him until his very pores let blood.

I know that history has provided the world with details of what happened next and it is painful to remember closely the details of His arrest and torture. And of His death. The cross that held the body so dear to me was to become the symbol of hope and life eternal for millions.

He forbade me to accompany him, and in truth I could not bear to witness His agony that night. I knew too, that so deep and all encompassing would be his anguish, he was not willing for me to witness it. To defy him would only add to the enormity of his burden. Had I known that even Peter would fall asleep while my beloved sweated blood from his very pores, I would have not been moved from his side.

Judas did his work that night, as Yeshua had foretold. Betraying my beloved with a kiss, he earned his silver and his place in black history, although Yeshua had tried to make me understand that he was merely playing out his part in what had been ordained.

His mother and John were with me as we witnessed his trial at Pilate's hands. Each stroke of the lash bit into our own hearts and as Mother Mary was near to collapse in her anguish and grief so too did I die a little inside, all we could do was to cling to each other as our grief became too big a burden to bear alone. How she bore her pain at Calvary with such dignity I will never know, I do know that I cried the tears of the lost and of the wife I had become and with each nail I died a little inside.

Joseph reclaimed His body and we took it for burial as was our custom. I had not finished the anointing when daylight went and we had to stop because of the Sabbath. I could hardly tear myself away and yet I knew He would not want me to violate that day.

I returned before daybreak on that Monday morning. Imagine my despair as I saw the tomb was open and that His body was gone. Panic overtook my reason and my understanding. They had taken Him away. I couldn't finish my precious task of anointing Him and so assist His Soul on its sacred journey. I had let Him down. Me, of all others, I had let Him down.

I sobbed uncontrollably and even when I saw the figure approach, I couldn't see through my river of tears who it was that drew near. I assumed it was the gardener, come to see who was weeping so loudly in a place of peace. I begged for Him to tell me where they had taken my Beloved and I would go to Him and claim Him.

Just one word, 'Mary,' he said.

Time stood still as my heart ceased its regular beating and I transcended reality and was transported with pain and joy to a place where my Beloved still walked. I reached up to gently touch His face, to feel Him with me once again and in that instant I felt the child within me move for the first time, she too responded to the pure joy of his presence.

'Rabounni,' I whispered, His name caught in my throat.

'You cannot cling to me, Beloved', he said, 'I have not yet ascended to my Father-Mother, you see me in the form of my light body.'

Minutes turned to hours as He taught me things about the Soul that I could only wonder at. He finished His teaching and gently blessed me.

'Go to the others,' He said, 'Tell them that I have risen, as I said I would, and that I will come to them before I return to my Father.'

I felt my heart would break if I left him but he was quietly insistent. I hated to leave Him but I went to the others as he had asked of me although they would not heed me. Peter had done his work well.

It was beyond their belief that our Lord had arisen from the grave, alive again, and that if it was true that he would choose to appear first to me, a mere woman despite our relationship. There was much dissent in that room and voices were raised in anger and fear and unbelief. Eventually they came with me and saw for themselves the empty tomb. My Lord came to us all in time and even Thomas, who had never believed without seeing, fell to the floor as he witnessed the wounds for himself as my Yeshua stood before him.

Before many days had passed he told us of his ascension and when we finally saw him rise into the heavens we knew he was gone from us forever in his physical form of Yeshua, but that he would remain with us forever as Christ, our Lord. He would remain with me always as my Beloved.

I tried so hard to fulfil my promise to him and comfort the others but met with an ever increasing hostility from Peter and some of the others who refused to believe that a woman could understand some of the higher teachings that were given. John understood, but his grief was so great he could not rouse himself to my defence, and his days were given to the comfort and care of Mother Mary.

Peter, as ever, was angry at my presumption and lost no time in alienating as many of the others as he could. I wept with hurt and frustration as they gathered themselves around him and cloaked themselves in their own comfortable version of the truth that missed the point completely. Was it all to be for nothing?

I continued to try and get through to them, to explain the deeper meanings of Yeshua's teachings, but to no avail, entrenched as they had become in the old beliefs in a new setting. John understood, but then he too had been close to our Master. He had the optimism of youth on his side and an insight that always made Yeshua smile.

The visions of Him began very soon after my Beloved ascended and continued to show the ways of the soul and of its ultimate ascension to become one with the Divine Light and I took comfort in the conversations our souls had together. Peter would not have any of it although Levi defended me, knowing I would not lie about such a thing.

Yeshua's uncle, Joseph of Arimathea came to me then, It was imperative, he said, for me to leave Jerusalem. If it were to become known that I had been His wife and I could no longer hide the child I carried, my life and hers could be in danger, the crowds were frenzied and the Roman army along with the Pharisees were looking for an easy way out. Enough blood had been spilled. What Joseph didn't know, was that Peter too had been a threat to me. In his shame and grief, I wasn't sure what he may do and I feared his temper.

John took Mother Mary to Antioch and I was hurried from the city and into Egypt. His child would be born in a foreign land, but a land with which we had both been familiar. After many months of travelling and teaching his truth to any who would listen to me I passed on what was written as the Gospel of Mary. This too was destined, like its author, to become hidden through fear and shame until it was found in its Coptic form at the time when mankind is ready to receive its truth.

I eventually arrived on the southern coast of France with Joseph and Lazarus and Martha. I was welcomed by these people who cared for me and looked to Yeshua's teachings. They accepted me for who I am and in time they cared for me as their own. Later down the centuries many would even die defending my truth against the might of the Roman Church. I would be defended by Knights and my secrets would be encoded in architecture and worship and art, though Peter's influence would become the cornerstone of the religion founded in my Beloved's name. So fearful of my truth were they that they would distort my history until I would be remembered as a prostitute and not a royal bride.

During the years after my flight I travelled many miles, reaching the Celtic land of Scotland where many churches and chapels sprang up in my name. I was bound for Iona, the holy isle, eventually to return to the southern coast of Gaul which you now call France. I retreated into the caves of St Baume and was visited daily by angels who brought the Holy Eucharist to sustain me. As my end approached, they took me to my old friend Bishop Maximin who gave me the last sacrament.

As on many occasions since his ascension, my Beloved came to me in a vision as I left my earthly form. He took my hand.

'Mary,' he said.

'Rabbounni', I whispered.

Enò Notes

So, I am now satisfied that my search for the feminine principle hidden within Christianity has led me to my own truth. Was Mary Magdalene indeed the true Bride of Christ? I believe so. Was she Goddess? Yes and No. In her humanity she became the opposite and complementary female energy to the human Yeshua, the consort and wife of the Christ, fully human but her connection with the archetypical Goddess figure is close enough to reunite the God/Goddess principles into the heart of Christianity. She was not divine as was Yeshua, but she truly embodied the Sacred Feminine in every aspect of her being, to make her worthy of reverence and acknowledgement as the Divine Feminine in humanity.

Did she bear a child fathered by Jesus? I believe so. Are the Merovingians the true bloodline of Christ? I don't know is the only true answer I can give. It's possible, even likely, and the Merovingian line and heritage will defend that as fact. But does it really matter? Any offspring of the union will also, like the mother be fully human and subject to the flaws and temptations of so being. I feel that as it is Christ only that

163

remains truly divine, the question of children remains subjective. Is it heresy or worse, blasphemy? For my part, the intention is neither. My deep and abiding love of Christ must now include, and it surely does, an intense love of the Magdalene.

It may seem that I have been overly critical of the established Church, both Anglican and Roman, but again I have only sought to find the truth. Thankfully, the years of oppression and censorship have diminished from within its ranks though it does still have far to go, especially with the election of a pope who is adamant that nothing will change and strives daily to perpetuate the travesty of denial of women from within its sacred halls. Rome, it seems remains determined to deny the Sacred Bride. I am in fact an ordained Christian Minister but not by a Church that denies the very existence of what can only be truth and beauty within its Sacred Feminine. In the days when orthodox churches are empty and boarded up, and seminaries devoid of students, we can foresee the death throes of the remnants of the patriarchal church, but from the ashes must rise the phoenix of truth and the real message of Christ at a time when we need it most.

Jesus was God in Man, the Son of God and His divinity is without question, but as the Son of God, who then are both parents? We know that the Virgin Mary received of the Holy Spirit and gave birth to the human form that hosted God on earth, but she too was human. The Goddess is to be found within the God, in Creation itself and I believe that we are being called at this time to understand and acknowledge that our origin and source is of a sacred union of both male and female in balance and harmony and when we can externalise that understanding into the world, we may have a hope of survival as mankind.

When all else falls away, Christ's teachings are that the Divine is within us all, and we can access true communion with the Divine at any time, but it is a divinity that is both male and female. When we live in and of love as Yeshua taught us, then, perhaps, this Earth will become the Kingdom that he taught us to expect and is in fact the true heritage of the Throne of David.

The pathway to spiritual revelation must lead us individually to the higher truth. It begins in one heart.
In each and every one of us.

May the peace and love of Christ and the Magdalene, be with you and remain with you unto the end of time, for God's sake.

And for ours.

Amen.

Bibliography

The Holy Bible, KJV & NIV

The Gospel of Mary, From the Nag Hammadi Library

The Gospel of Phillip, From the Nag Hammadi Library

The Gospel of Thomas , From the Nag Hammadi Library

The Dialogue of the Saviour, From the Nag Hammadi Library

The Secret Teachings of Jesus , Marvin W Meyer (Translated by) 1986

Pistis Sophia, G R S Mead

The Nag Hammadi Library, James M Robinson 1978 (Edited by)

The Woman with the Alabaster Jar, Margaret Starbird 1993

The Holy Land of Scotland, Barry Dunford

The Bloodline of the Holy Grail, Lawrence Gardner 1988

Mary Magdalene, Lynne Picknett 1988

The Goddess in the Gospels, Margaret Starbird 1998

The Gospel of Mary Magdalene, Jean Yves LeLoup 1997

Mary Magdalene: First Apostle, Anne Graham Brock 2003

Prayers for the Cosmos, Neil Douglas-Klotz 1994

The Key to the Sacred Pattern, Henry Lincoln 1997

The Holy Blood and Holy Grail, Michael Baigent et al. 1982

The Church of Mary Magdalene, Jean Markale 2004

FREE DETAILED CATALOGUE

Capall Bann is owned and run by people actively involved in many of the areas in which we publish. A detailed illustrated catalogue is available on request, SAE or International Postal Coupon appreciated. **Titles can be ordered direct from Capall Bann, post free in the UK** (cheque or PO with order) or from good bookshops and specialist outlets.

A Breath Behind Time, Terri Hector
A Soul is Born by Eleyna Williamson
Angels and Goddesses - Celtic Christianity & Paganism, M. Howard
The Art of Conversation With the Genius Loci, Barry Patterson
Arthur - The Legend Unveiled, C Johnson & E Lung
Astrology The Inner Eye - A Guide in Everyday Language, E Smith
Auguries and Omens - The Magical Lore of Birds, Yvonne Aburrow
Asyniur - Womens Mysteries in the Northern Tradition, S McGrath
Beginnings - Geomancy, Builder's Rites in the European Tradition, Nigel Pennick
Between Earth and Sky, Julia Day
Book of the Veil , Peter Paddon
The Book of Seidr, Runic John
Caer Sidhe - Celtic Astrology and Astronomy, Michael Bayley
Call of the Horned Piper, Nigel Jackson
Can't Sleep, Won't Sleep, Linga Louisa Dell
Carnival of the Animals, Gregor Lamb
Cat's Company, Ann Walker
Celtic Faery Shamanism, Catrin James
Celtic Lore & Druidic Ritual, Rhiannon Ryall
Celtic Sacrifice - Pre Christian Ritual & Religion, Marion Pearce
Celtic Saints and the Glastonbury Zodiac, Mary Caine
Circle and the Square, Jack Gale
Come Back To Life, Jenny Smedley
Creating Form From the Mist - The Wisdom of Women in Celtic Myth and
    Culture, Lynne Sinclair-Wood
Crystal Clear - A Guide to Quartz Crystal, Jennifer Dent
Crystal Doorways, Simon & Sue Lilly
Crossing the Borderlines - Guising, Masking & Ritual Animal Disguise in the
    European Tradition, Nigel Pennick
Dragons of the West, Nigel Pennick
Earth Dance - A Year of Pagan Rituals, Jan Brodie
Earth Harmony - Places of Power, Holiness & Healing, Nigel Pennick
Earth Magic, Margaret McArthur

Egyptian Animals - Guardians & Gateways of the Gods, Akkadia Ford
Eildon Tree (The) Romany Language & Lore, Michael Hoadley
Enchanted Forest - The Magical Lore of Trees, Yvonne Aburrow
Eternal Priestess, Sage Weston
Eternally Yours Faithfully, Roy Radford & Evelyn Gregory
Everything You Always Wanted To Know About Your Body, But So Far
        Nobody's Been Able To Tell You, Chris Thomas & D Baker
Experiencing the Green Man, Rob Hardy & Teresa Moorey
Fairies and Nature Spirits, Teresa Moorey
Fairies in the Irish Tradition, Molly Gowen
Familiars - Animal Powers of Britain, Anna Franklin
Flower Wisdom, Katherine Kear
Fool's First Steps, (The) Chris Thomas
Forest Paths - Tree Divination, Brian Harrison, Ill. S. Rouse
From Past to Future Life, Dr Roger Webber
Gardening For Wildlife Ron Wilson
God Year, The, Nigel Pennick & Helen Field
Goddess on the Cross, Dr George Young
Goddess Year, The, Nigel Pennick & Helen Field
Goddesses, Guardians & Groves, Jack Gale
Handbook For Pagan Healers, Liz Joan
Handbook of Fairies, Ronan Coghlan
Healing Book, The, Chris Thomas and Diane Baker
Healing Homes, Jennifer Dent
Healing Journeys, Paul Williamson
Healing Stones, Sue Philips
Herb Craft - Shamanic & Ritual Use of Herbs, Lavender & Franklin
Hidden Heritage - Exploring Ancient Essex, Terry Johnson
In Search of Herne the Hunter, Eric Fitch
In Search of the Green Man, Peter Hill
Inner Celtia, Alan Richardson & David Annwn
Inner Mysteries of the Goths, Nigel Pennick
Inner Space Workbook - Develop Thru Tarot, C Summers & J Vayne
Intuitive Journey, Ann Walker Isis - African Queen, Akkadia Ford
Journey Home, The, Chris Thomas
Kecks, Keddles & Kesh - Celtic Lang & The Cog Almanac, Bayley
Language of the Psycards, Berenice
Legend of Robin Hood, The, Richard Rutherford-Moore
Lid Off the Cauldron, Patricia Crowther
Light From the Shadows - Modern Traditional Witchcraft, Gwyn
Lore of the Sacred Horse, Marion Davies
Lost Lands & Sunken Cities (2nd ed.), Nigel Pennick
Magic For the Next 1,000 Years, Jack Gale
Magic of Herbs - A Complete Home Herbal, Rhiannon Ryall
Magical Guardians - Exploring the Spirit and Nature of Trees, Philip Heselton
Magical History of the Horse, Janet Farrar & Virginia Russell

Magical Lore of Animals, Yvonne Aburrow
Magical Lore of Cats, Marion Davies
Magical Lore of Herbs, Marion Davies
Magick Without Peers, Ariadne Rainbird & David Rankine
Masks of Misrule - Horned God & His Cult in Europe, Nigel Jackson
Medium Rare - Reminiscences of a Clairvoyant, Muriel Renard
Mind Massage - 60 Creative Visualisations, Marlene Maundrill
Mirrors of Magic - Evoking the Spirit of the Dewponds, P Heselton
The Moon and You, Teresa Moorey
Moon Mysteries, Jan Brodie
Mysteries of the Runes, Michael Howard
Mystic Life of Animals, Ann Walker
New Celtic Oracle The, Nigel Pennick & Nigel Jackson
Oracle of Geomancy, Nigel Pennick
Pagan Feasts - Seasonal Food for the 8 Festivals, Franklin & Phillips
Patchwork of Magic - Living in a Pagan World, Julia Day
Pathworking - A Practical Book of Guided Meditations, Pete Jennings
Personal Power, Anna Franklin
Pickingill Papers - The Origins of Gardnerian Wicca, Bill Liddell
Pillars of Tubal Cain, Nigel Jackson
Places of Pilgrimage and Healing, Adrian Cooper
Planet Earth - The Universe's Experiment, Chris Thomas
Practical Divining, Richard Foord
Practical Meditation, Steve Hounsome
Practical Spirituality, Steve Hounsome
Psychic Self Defence - Real Solutions, Jan Brodie
Real Fairies, David Tame
Reality - How It Works & Why It Mostly Doesn't, Rik Dent
Romany Tapestry, Michael Houghton
Runic Astrology, Nigel Pennick
Sacred Animals, Gordon MacLellan
Sacred Celtic Animals, Marion Davies, Ill. Simon Rouse
Sacred Dorset - On the Path of the Dragon, Peter Knight
Sacred Grove - The Mysteries of the Forest, Yvonne Aburrow
Sacred Geometry, Nigel Pennick
Sacred Nature, Ancient Wisdom & Modern Meanings, A Cooper
Sacred Ring - Pagan Origins of British Folk Festivals, M. Howard
Season of Sorcery - On Becoming a Wisewoman, Poppy Palin
Seasonal Magic - Diary of a Village Witch, Paddy Slade
Secret Places of the Goddess, Philip Heselton
Secret Signs & Sigils, Nigel Pennick
The Secrets of East Anglian Magic, Nigel Pennick
A Seeker's Guide To Past Lives, Paul Williamson
Seeking Pagan Gods, Teresa Moorey
Self Enlightenment, Mayan O'Brien
Spirits of the Earth series, Jaq D Hawkins

Stony Gaze, Investigating Celtic Heads John Billingsley
Stumbling Through the Undergrowth , Mark Kirwan-Heyhoe
Subterranean Kingdom, The, revised 2nd ed, Nigel Pennick
Symbols of Ancient Gods, Rhiannon Ryall
Talking to the Earth, Gordon MacLellan
Talking With Nature, Julie Hood
Taming the Wolf - Full Moon Meditations, Steve Hounsome
Teachings of the Wisewomen, Rhiannon Ryall
The Other Kingdoms Speak, Helena Hawley
Transformation of Housework, Ben Bushill
Tree: Essence of Healing, Simon & Sue Lilly
Tree Seer, Simon & Sue Lilly
Understanding Chaos Magic, Jaq D Hawkins
Understanding Past Lives, Dilys Gater
Understanding Second Sight, Dilys Gater
Understanding Spirit Guides, Dilys Gater
Understanding Star Children, Dilys Gater
The Urban Shaman, Dilys Gater
Vortex - The End of History, Mary Russell
Warp and Weft - In Search of the I-Ching, William de Fancourt
Warriors at the Edge of Time, Jan Fry
Water Witches, Tony Steele
Way of the Magus, Michael Howard
Weaving a Web of Magic, Rhiannon Ryall
West Country Wicca, Rhiannon Ryall
What's Your Poison? vol 1, Tina Tarrant
Wheel of the Year, Teresa Moorey & Jane Brideson
Wildwitch - The Craft of the Natural Psychic, Poppy Palin
Wildwood King , Philip Kane
A Wisewoman's Book of Tea Leaf Reading, Pat Barki
The Witch's Kitchen, Val Thomas
Wondrous Land - The Faery Faith of Ireland by Dr Kay Mullin
Working With Crystals, Shirley o'Donoghue
Working With Natural Energy, Shirley o'Donoghue
Working With the Merlin, Geoff Hughes
Your Talking Pet, Ann Walker